GREAT ★ ★ ★
GOVERNMENT
GOOFS!

Books by the author

GREAT GOVERNMENT GOOFS!
PRESUMED IGNORANT!
PRESIDENTIAL INDISCRETIONS

GREAT ★ ★ ★ GOVERNMENT GOOFS!

Over 350 Loopy Laws, Hilarious Screwups,
and Acts-idents of Congress

LELAND H. GREGORY, III

A DELL TRADE PAPERBACK

A DELL TRADE PAPERBACK
Published by
Dell Publishing
a division of
Random House, Inc.
1540 Broadway
New York, New York 10036

Library of Congress Cataloging in Publication Data
Gregory, Leland.
   Great government goofs! over 350 loopy laws, hilarious screwups, and acts-idents of Congress / by Leland H. Gregory III.
     p.   cm.
   ISBN 0-440-50786-3
   1. Bureaucracy—United States—Humor. 2. Waste in government spending—United States—Humor. I. Title.
JK421G77 1997
351'.02'07—dc21   97-9109
                                               CIP

Printed in the United States of America

Published simultaneously in Canada

November 1997

10 9 8 7 6 5 4

BVG

This book is dedicated to my wife, Gloria, for her love, talent, guidance, understanding, and encouragement. Your help with this manuscript has once again fooled everyone into believing that I am the writer in the family. Thank you for who you are.

ACKNOWLEDGMENTS

If you can't laugh at yourself who can you laugh at? *Great Government Goofs! Over 350 Loopy Laws, Hilarious Screwups, and Acts-idents of Congress* shouldn't be considered a manifesto against our government; since the government is made up of people, this book is about human folly and the silliness some people get into in their pursuit of power. However, the only way to stop a lot of Washington waste, pork-barrel legislation, back-room dealings, and unethical behavior of the men and women we elect to public office is to be aware that these things exist—and let them know we know.

The author would like to thank the people from the following organizations who were invaluable in helping gather stories: the National Performance Review, General Accounting Office, EPA Watch, Competitive Enterprise Institute, Hartland Institute, Heritage Foundation, Cato Institute, State Department Watch, and the National Taxpayers Union. I would like to send out a personal thank-you to the great people at the Citizens Against Government Waste—your advice, information, and knowledge helped more than you know.

Thanks to my agent, Jonathon Lazear, and all the people at the Lazear Agency; to Al Franken, who is totally unaware of the role he played in getting this book to publication; and to Kathleen Jayes, my editor at Dell.

I would also like to thank all the men and women who screwed up enough to be included in this book.

Calendar of Events

Because of the Veterans Day holiday next Wednesday, this release will be published on Friday, November 13, instead of on Thursday, November 12. It will be issued on Thursday, November 19, its usual publication date, but will be delayed the following week until Friday, November 27, because of the Thanksgiving Day holiday on Thursday, November 26.
—Federal Reserve memo

"All you need to know is this. You can never go wrong voting for a bill that fails, or against a bill that passes."
—Senator Robert Dole (R-Kansas)

Bush-Whacked

President Nixon made important breakthroughs in relations between the United States and China; President Carter made important breakthroughs between Egypt and Israel; and President Bush made his breakthrough in Japan, in a big way. While dining with Japan's Prime Minister, Kiichi Miyazawa, George Bush (forty-first President) gave etiquette the old heave-ho when he heave-hoed his dinner all over Prime Minister Miyazawa's shoes. The President's faux-pas gave Japan one of its newest words: *Bushusuru*. The usually reserved Japanese now have a socially accepted verb for the act of "losing your lunch." Bushusuru quickly made its way into Japanese magazines, television shows, even a trained monkey act. When the monkey hears the word "*Bushusuru!*" it imitates President Bush throwing up on Prime Minister Miyazawa; the act is accompanied with realistic sound effects. And some said Bush wasn't good at loosening up around foreign dignitaries.

Alaska State Senator Bob Ziegler
introduced a bill to make it illegal for a
civilian dog to impersonate a police dog.

See Ya Later, Alligator

Members of the Georgia State Game Commission were fiercely debating the pros and cons of regulating "alligator *rides*" when one alert member noticed a typographical error on the agenda—the commission was actually supposed to be discussing whether or not they should regulate "alligator *hides*."

Congress approved $500,000 for the reconstruction of the home of Charles Corneau—who was simply Abraham Lincoln's neighbor.

The Cola Wars

Soldiers have historically faced mortar rounds, bullets, bayonets, mines, tanks, missiles, and even hand-to-hand combat. But there's a new enemy on the horizon, lurking in the halls of barracks and PXs on every base. A report on these six-foot armored antipersonnel devices was issued in a 1988 issue of the *Journal of the American Medical Association*. Dr. Michael Cosio of the Walter Reed Army Medical Center investigated fifteen instances in which servicemen (no women) engaged unsuccessfully in hand-to-lever combat with adversarial soda machines. The study showed that in "case after case" servicemen trying to wrangle a free pop, or angry over the machine stealing their money, tilted, rocked, and shook the thousand-pound machines, which promptly fell on them. Three died and twelve had to be hospitalized due to this "fizzy friendly fire." Cosio also investigated thirty-two incidents of civilian soda machine unrest, which resulted in twenty-four injuries and eight deaths of nonservice personnel. The combat manual has a section on dealing with chemical warfare—but nothing about carbonated warfare. The battle rages on.

"I haven't committed a crime. What I did
was fail to comply with the law."
—*New York City Mayor David Dinkins,*
on accusations that he failed to pay his taxes

I Didn't Even Know They Were Sick

Everyone in Hartford, Connecticut, is dead! At least according to computer records. During an investigation in the mid-1980s into why Hartford's residents had been excluded from federal grand juries for three years, it was discovered that a computer error had listed everyone in town as being dead. Why? The city's name had been inputted into the wrong section of the records, forcing the *d* in Hartford into the column on jury information. So whenever the random jury selection chose someone from Hartford, the computer recognized the *d* in the information column as meaning "Dead." And since Hartford is the insurance capitol of the world, makes you wonder how many life insurance policies were cashed in.

"With incest, you could get super-smart kids."
—*Representative Carl Gunter (R-Louisiana)*

A Tisket,
A Tasket,
A Profitable Casket

It makes sense that Supplemental Security Income and Medicaid benefits are reduced when a person has extra money coming in or "profitable assets." Things like stocks and bonds are understand-able—but a coffin! Ninety-year-old Altona Brown's coffin, which she bought in advance for $2,946, was not considered a "burial receptacle" by the federal government but was listed as a "profitable asset." In 1993 Ms. Brown, an Athabaskan Indian, was denied $30 a month in Social Security and all Medicaid benefits because the Social Security office claimed Brown's coffin was too extravagant to be considered as an exempt "burial receptacle." They demanded she sell the coffin, along with the skin mittens, rugs, $700 plane ticket (to fly her body to her final resting place), and beaded moccasins she had painstakingly hand-crafted as part of a Native American burial ritual. Ms. Brown, who is blind, was denied Medicaid and ran up $60,000 in debt at the Fairbanks, Alaska, nursing home where she lives. Protests and public outcry finally caused the government to withdraw its claim against Ms. Brown in December 1994, allowing her to keep her coffin and her burial outfit and reinstating her Medicaid. Wasn't that nice of them? You can rest in peace . . . as long as the government gets its piece first.

☆

$500,000 authorized by Congress to construct a replica of Egypt's Great Pyramid—in Indiana.

Getting Behind the Law

Laws need to be specific so authorities know exactly who's doing wrong and who's doing right—and they don't arrest the wrong people, I mean the right people—the people in the right (see what I mean?). Anyway, no need to worry if you're in St. Augustine, Florida, because they regulate nudity on beaches and in restaurants—and they know a naked person when they see one. The following is taken from a St. Augustine, Florida, ordinance prohibiting exposure of, well, you'll see.

> *Buttocks: The area at the rear of the human body (sometimes referred to as the gluteus maximus) which lies between two imaginary lines running parallel to the ground when a person is standing, the first or top of such line being one-half inch below the top of the vertical cleavage of the nates (i.e., the prominence formed by the muscles running from the back of the hip to the back of the leg) and the second or bottom line being one-half inch about the lowest point of curvature of the fleshy protuberance (sometimes referred to as the gluteal fold), and between two imaginary lines, one on each side of the body (the "outside lines"), which outside lines are perpendicular to the ground and to the horizontal lines described above and which perpendicular outside lines pass through the outermost point(s) at which each nate meets the outer side of each leg. . . .*

You can rest assured of two things; one, authorities will know a butt when they come face-to-face with it; and two, the author of this ordinance will never get a job writing romance novels.

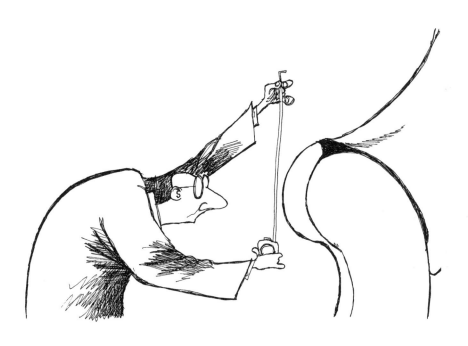

No Strike Zone

During the 1980s, in a bold stroke against terrorism, the Chico, California, City Council banned nuclear weapons, enacting a mandatory $500 fine for anyone detonating a nuclear weapon within city limits. The question is, who would be around to collect?

According to Vice President Al Gore's book *Common Sense Government* (1995), the Defense Department spends more on procedures for travel reimbursement ($2.2 billion) than on travel ($2 billion).

"Things are more like they are now than they have ever been."

—*Gerald Ford (Thirty-eighth President)*

Button, Button, Who's Got the Button?

For Kids' Sake, Think Toy Safety was the motto displayed on 80,000 buttons designed and distributed in 1974 by the Consumer Product Safety Commission. The buttons had to be recalled because they could be accidentally swallowed, the pinpoint was too sharp, and the paint was toxic. The taxpayers need to print up their own buttons: For Our Sake, Think!

Myrtle Beach, South Carolina, city officials, announced that the city's yellow water is safe to drink, although it stains laundry.

The Check's in the Mail

Most businesses pay quarterly taxes and there are stiff penalties for being late. So imagine the surprise on the faces of thousands of Washington, D.C., business owners who mailed their corporate taxes in time for the September 30, 1994, deadline only to have them returned "Box Closed for Nonpayment of Rent." The post office box the city used to collect corporate taxes had been closed since June, according to district officials, because the city never coughed up the $405 annual fee. The city claimed it wasn't at fault because the post office never sent them a reminder that the rent for the box was delinquent. That's a scary thought—the government waiting for a reminder from the post office.

In 1989 Congress supplied the Pentagon with $49,000 to discover if members of the armed forces would spend money on military lottery tickets.

Luck of the Draw

1994 was a tough election year for many politicians. But no race was tougher than the one for city council in Rice, Minnesota. Virgil Nelson and Mitch Fiedler ran a head-to-head race throughout the general election: it would be close. And it was. The vote tallied up ninety for Nelson and ninety for Fiedler, a tie. These two fine politicians decided to allow their futures to be "in the cards." On the first draw, both drew eights. They drew again. This time they both drew aces. Finally, on the third draw, Nelson drew a seven and Fielder finished him off with an eight. Fielder was victorious and assumed the position of city council member. I can see his campaign slogan for next year: "Mitch Fiedler. A 'cut' above the rest."

NASA spent $200,000 to develop a sweet potato that can be grown in outer space.

Coin Laundry

New York City had a problem. The private company hired to collect money from city parking meters had been stealing them blind, a quarter at a time—to the tune of $1 million. So the city's transportation department decided to form a sixty-one-member parking meter service unit in 1987 that would put a halt to this "small change" theft. The private company was fired and the fine men and women of the new parking meter service were put to the task of collecting an estimated $47 million in revenue each year from the city's 67,000 parking meters. But six years later, it's déjà vu all over again. Twenty members of the meter service were arrested and charged with stealing over $1 million in quarters over the previous two years. City investigators said that one third of the staff had been stealing up to $1,500 in coins each. The "loose change" artists would secretly stash away hundreds of quarters at a time and conceal them in canvas bags they carried with them. One "coin collector" bragged to an undercover city investigator that he had stolen $45,000 in two years—or $5,625 per quarter (sorry, I couldn't help myself). City inspector Ellen Schwartz was quoted in *The New York Times* as saying, "Within those five hours, they were able to steal the money, place the quarters in paper rolls, drop off the money at their homes or convert the quarters into currency at banks, and still find time to go to the office and play cards." And you thought government employees were lazy!

"Outside of the killings, we have one of the lowest crime rates in the country."

—*Washington, D.C., Mayor Marion Barry*

Governing Beyond the Grave

Your food stamps will be stopped effective March 1992 because we received notice that you passed away. May God bless you. You may reapply if there is a change in your circumstances.

—Notice from Greenville, South Carolina, County Department of Social Services

"It's not like molesting young girls or
young boys. It's not a showstopper."

—*Texas Congressman Charlie Wilson, underplaying his bouncing
eighty-one checks at the House of Representatives bank,
including one to the IRS—for $6,500*

The Real Playboy Bunnies

In 1980 the Wyoming legislature passed a piece of landmark legislation on the issue of invasion of privacy—they banned taking photographs of rabbits from January through April without an official permit. If you want to take a shot of one of these furry woodland creatures, it had better be with a gun.

"People are more interested in a strong economy than someone who can tell you if Hootie and the Blowfish are going to have a strong album next time."

—*Dole press secretary Nelson Warfield in 1995, on why being hip won't be an issue for candidates in the 1996 presidential contest*

Fair Warning and Forewarning

Texas State Representative Jim Kaster introduced a bill into the state legislature that would require anyone who plans on committing a crime to give their would-be victim at least twenty-four hours notice. This notice could be given orally (over the phone or in person), or in writing and must also inform the intended victim that it's okay to use deadly force as a defense—but only in certain crimes. Can you imagine:

> "Dear Jim,
> On Tuesday, January 14, around 10:43 or 10:45 P.M., depending on traffic, I will rob you using an unloaded gun. If you catch me you are allowed to kick my butt; however, since the gun is unloaded, you can't kill me.
> Sincerely,
> Charles 'The Stupidest Criminal in the World' Thompson."

In 1987 Mississippi Representative Will Green Poindexter introduced a bill into the state legislature that would give dwarfs permission to use crossbows to hunt deer during archery season.

Two Months out of the Year

During the energy crisis of the late 1970s, thousands of people came up with creative ways to save energy: car pooling, sharing a shower, using low-watt bulbs. But Ohio State Representative John Galbraith came up with the most timely suggestion. He introduced a bill to eliminate January and February from the calendar. His thinking went like this: "If we divided the fifty-nine extra days between July and August, we will cut our energy needs by about one third through eliminating the coldest days of the year. Cold is largely a psychological matter. If people look at the calendar and see that it is July, they will be quite happy to turn the heat down." Looking at his reasoning, it's safe to say that Representative Galbraith isn't just two months shy of a year—he's two cards shy of a full deck.

Congress allocated $19 million to examine the amount of methane gas emitted from cow flatulence.

Permission Slips

In another case of "Put It in Writing," Oklahoma State Representative Cleta Deatherage introduced a bill that would require men to obtain advance written permission from any female with whom they wish to have sexual intercourse. The man must give the woman a written notice that also makes clear that having sex could cause pregnancy in the female, and could be hazardous to her health. If the man wants to have sex with a woman who is illiterate, or for any reason can't read the statement, the warnings must be read to her in her native language. Again:

> "Dear Janice,
> On Tuesday, January 14, around 10:43 or 10:45, depending on traffic, and continuing until 10:47 or 10:48, depending on me, I wish to have sexual intercourse with you using a loaded weapon . . ." et cetera, et cetera.

> The bill was defeated.

$9,720,000 added by the House for the Jacksonville Automated Skyway Express (SDE) extension project. The projected cost of this project is $34 million per mile—and is considered by the Department of Transportation as "an amusement ride."

Lost in the Wilderness Act

July 12, 1994: The Pecos Wilderness Mountains of northern New Mexico were alive with the laughter and singing of Boy Scout Troop 42 from Lake Bluff, Illinois. As they hiked along a trail, fourteen-year-old Robert Graham II became sidetracked and took a different path, accidentally separating from the rest of his troop. His backpack held only a sleeping bag, a small tent, and a box of gingersnaps. Darkness fell on the remote mountains and soon Robert was lost. All alone, he made camp in an open space, confident that a rescue team would find him. He waited.

July 14, 1994: Robert heard the sounds of a helicopter and his heart leapt into his throat. Frantically he waved his arms to get the pilot's attention. The chopper closed the distance slowly, circled the air around Robert's makeshift camp, and then flew away. Robert couldn't understand why the helicopter didn't land in the open meadow.

Later that afternoon, in Santa Fe, New Mexico, the St. John's College Search and Rescue team received a call from the New Mexico State Police requesting rescue assistance for a lost Boy Scout. The report stated that a police helicopter pilot had spotted the young boy in a meadow and had been denied permission to land by the U.S. Forest Service. Why? Because the U.S. Forest Service is a department of our federal government, and according to a law hidden deep in the Wilderness Act of 1964, motorized vehicles are not allowed in federal wilderness areas unless "required in emergencies involving the health and safety of persons in the area." It would seem this act was written exclusively to help someone in Robert's situation. But a representative of the Forest Service rescue squad explained that because the boy was able to wave his arms, he must be all right. Therefore, it was no emergency. Since the rescue wasn't allowed to take place by air, the only alternative was a ground rescue. According to Herb Kincey, who has led volunteer search-and-rescue missions for thirty years, the twenty-mile hike up and back down the treacherous mountain would take up to sixteen hours to accomplish—whereas a helicopter rescue would take minutes. "This is ridiculous," Kincey, the founder of the St. John's rescue team, said. "How much environmental damage would be done by a helicopter landing for five minutes, as opposed to ten people slashing their way for miles though the area?" After agonizing over the situation, Kincey and his St. John's team refused to attempt the rescue on the Forest Service's ridiculous terms. Confident that their way was the right way, Forest Services dispatched their own ground rescue team. After only six hours, their team gave up. They failed to find Robert, even though his location had been plotted and mapped. Finally the government approved a helicopter rescue.

July 15, 1994: Flying over the meadow in a U.S. Customs Service helicopter, Kincey saw the boy still camped out. It took only minutes for little Robert to climb aboard the helicopter and fly to safety—after having waited, alone, hungry, and frightened for more than fifty hours while federal bureaucrats played games with his life.

In 1995 the Tennessee House of Representatives voted to make the Tennessee cave salamander the official state amphibian.

Catapulted to the White House

In 1986 Morris the Cat, the infamous finicky eater, tried to scratch his way onto the ballot for Democratic nominee for President of the United States. According to his communications director, "The world is going to the dogs. America needs a President with courage, but one who won't pussyfoot around with the issues of peace—a President who when adversity arises will always land on his feet." Even though it was (hopefully) a publicity stunt, Morris the Cat got some help from some heavy hitters, including the daughter of former Vice President Walter Mondale. "Morris," she said, "says he intends on being the first feline, and he's jumping into this candidacy with four paws. He wants it to be known he has undertaken to uphold high moral standards and promises there will be no nights on the tiles." Morris failed to get the nomination—but probably could have done a better job than Dukakis (Michael not Kitty).

"If Lincoln were alive today, he'd roll over in his grave."

—*Gerald Ford (Thirty-eighth President)*

The Rath meat-packing plant, a privately owned business in Waterloo, Iowa, received $2.5 million to have asbestos removed courtesy of Senator Tom Harkin (D-Iowa).

Poetry in Motion

Richard Nixon played the piano, Bill Clinton the saxophone—politicians have creative sparks just like the rest of us. Some are writers, painters, dancers, or poets. In fact, in 1993, California state assemblyman William J. Knight was so proud of a poem he wrote, he decided to distribute it to fellow legislators. We'll call it "Bigotry Smigotry."

> *We have hobby, it's called "breeding,"*
> *Welfare pays for baby feeding.*
> *Kids need dentist? Wife need pills?*
> *We get free, we got no bills.*
> *We think America damn good place,*
> *Too damn good for white man's race.*
> *If they no like us, they can go,*
> *Got lots of room in Mexico.*

At least it rhymes!

☆

In 1995 the New York State Assembly had to recess after being unable to find hotel rooms— Grateful Dead concert-goers had booked them all.

Fill in the Blank

During a special session of the Texas legislature in 1989, Lonnie "Bo" Pilgrim, a well-known chicken magnate, handed out blank, but signed, $10,000 checks to members of the Texas legislature. The special session concerned worker compensation legislation, something in which Pilgrim had a special interest. Pilgrim admitted the checks weren't chicken feed but denied they were bribes—he insists they were just a clever way to achieve "name recognition." What do the law books say about such blatant special-interest gift giving? It's illegal during regular sessions of the legislature, but it's okay during special sessions. Another case of Fill-in-the-blank government.

In March 1995 the Hawaiian legislature debated whether to make the official state fish the *o'opu* or the *humuhumunukunukuapua'a*.

Scrooged by the Law

The 1992 holiday season was approaching Chicago. The weather was turning crisp, smiles returned to people's faces, and the city prepared for the year-end celebrations. The Sheraton Chicago Hotel & Towers renewed its annual tradition of asking its operators to greet callers with a cheery "Happy holidays." Sounds like a harmless way to celebrate the diverse holidays that occur around December. So imagine the surprise when one operator, Ninette Smith, informed her supervisors the greeting violated her religious beliefs. "We were surprised and puzzled," said the Sheraton's Ellen Butler. "Happy holidays is a standard generic greeting in business."

Smith told the Sheraton they could stick a stocking in it and went to the U.S. Equal Employment Opportunity Commission, claiming she was laid off after refusing to say, "Happy holidays." The hotel's stand is that Smith asked for a leave of absence. In the spirit of the season, the Sheraton gave Smith her job back and suggested Smith say, "Greetings," instead of "Happy holidays." But Smith roasted the Sheraton's chestnuts again and claimed that "Greetings" violated her rights too.

Smith went back to work for the Sheraton, who placed her in another position that is looked upon as a promotion. But the EEOC sued the Sheraton anyway. In December of 1993 both parties reached a settlement in which Smith received $1,250 in back pay and $2,500 in compensatory damages.

How could saying the word *Greetings* possibly violate an operator's rights? The EEOC's regional attorney, John Hendrickson, said, "They only wanted her to say it during the hotel's observation of the holiday season, so it is a violation." God bless us, every one!

$36,749,000 added by the House for a generic increase for industrial preparedness. What this means is unclear.

The Road Less Traveled

In the late 1980s the town of Grantham, New Hampshire, had two streets called Stoney Brook; Stoney Brook Drive and Stoney Brook Lane. Imagine how confusing this was for residents, let alone visitors. So, the town council decided to remedy the situation by changing the street names. The new names are Old Springs Drive and Old Springs Lane. I'm sure the residents of Grantham have a few new names for their town council.

"[I] was provided with additional input that was radically different from the truth. I assisted in furthering that version."
—*Lieutenant Colonel Oliver North, explaining his role in the Iran-Contra affair; July 1990*

Pulse Tone Phone

Grand Junction, Colorado, closed its suicide-prevention hot line due to budget cuts, and referred callers to another number. Upon calling the second number, suicidal persons were informed the call would cost twenty-five cents for the first minute and $2.50 for each minute after that. If they think they were depressed before, wait until they get their phone bill.

☆

In the fiscal year 1996 budget, **Congress approved $1,214,000 for potato research. Since 1983, $13,010,000 has been appropriated for such research.**

That Old Black Magic

Senator Matthew Feldman introduced a bill into the New Jersey Senate that would set a $1,000 fine and six months in jail for anyone who profited from selling and guaranteeing a "curse." The bill would punish anyone who placed a curse on a person's enemy by use of voodoo, "bones," demons, the "evil eye," or chanting magic words with the sole intention of bringing bad luck down on someone. The bill doesn't place a fine on the person paying for the services of a "witch doctor"—it only punishes the person placing the curse. Check your calendar, Senator, it's the 1990s not the 1660s.

All seven Democratic candidates, including six incumbents, in Rhode Island's 1995 local elections missed the deadline to nominate themselves to run for office.

100 Watts—100 Votes

Campaign reform is a big debate issue. We're all amazed at the amount of money spent on the 1996 presidential campaign and agree that something should be done about it. But what about the little guy, the small-town politician who has trouble getting people to turn out at the polls? In Bishopville, South Carolina, Representative Grady Brown outspent his opponent by nearly four to one during the 1994 primary campaign. Did he spend all his money on television and radio ads? Nope. He spent some of it to enlighten certain residents in his voting district—he paid their utility bills with campaign funds. Brown admits to helping with utility bills for "four or five years" and doesn't see anything wrong with this kind of political assistance. "That's just part of small-town politics," Brown says. "I've probably given out thousands of dollars over the past five years. A person is not going to vote for you for that reason." If Brown really believes that, his pilot light has gone out.

"Premature impact of an aircraft with terrain."

—*FAA term for* airplane crash

Is It Hot in Here or Am I Crazy?

The air in death chambers is usually stifling—it's supposed to be. But thanks to the Virginia Corrections Department, the air has become a bit easier to breathe. They've installed air-conditioning in the death chamber. Said one corrections official, "It makes it more comfortable for everybody." At least you can't accuse them of cruel and unusual punishment.

☆

Until recently, the U.S. government routinely paid $54 for an ordinary office stapler. Four dollars for the stapler—$50 for paperwork and overhead.

Oils Well That Ends Well

Laredo, Texas, oilman Tony Sanchez, Jr., a former Texas Parks and Wildlife commissioner, claimed his right to operate oil wells on state park land by stating, "There would be no greater joy than to see a beautiful park that our children and adults can go to and learn about the oil and gas industry." I can see it now, the WD-40 State Park.

"I think the free-enterprise system is
absolutely too important to be left to
the voluntary action of the marketplace."
—*U.S. Representative Richard Kelly (D-Florida), who was later
convicted for taking bribes in the 1970s Abscam scandal*

It's Your Mess— You Clean It Up

Drugs are illegal. So it makes sense to be fined for selling a bag of marijuana, a bag of cocaine, or a bag of any other narcotic—but to be fined $3,500 for selling a bag of dog chow? It happened to Russ Zimmer of Torrington, Wyoming. Zimmer's crime started when he accepted two checks from Torrington Hide and Metal, a battery salvaging plant. Zimmer, who runs a feed mill, received a check for $4.85 in 1984 for a bag of seed and a second check in 1977 for a bag of dog chow. Torrington Hide and Metal became victim of the Superfund Law—which is designed to make polluters financially responsible for cleaning up their mess. The Environmental Protection Agency brought action against them in 1991, and ordered them to "clean up their act." Instead of cleaning up their act, they cleaned out their offices and declared bankruptcy. Since the EPA couldn't get Torrington, they set their sights a notch lower and sued the five largest companies that contributed to the polluted site. Four of those five companies, in turn, sued fifty-four third parties identified as "potential contributors" to the mess to help pay the $1.25 million cleanup fine the EPA was demanding. This is where Russ Zimmer entered the picture. Because his name appeared on two canceled checks, he fell into the category of the "third parties." Others in that category included St. Joseph Children's Home and a South Dakota volunteer fire department.

➤

"They sued every company in town, in some cases without any evidence," says a furious Carol Browner, head of the EPA. Attorneys representing the third parties encouraged their clients to pay $500,000 as their share of the fine instead of going to court. Zimmer is in a Superfund super funk. "I blame Congress," he says. "They're the ones who allowed this to become law. They should straighten it out." But Congress is a lot like Torrington Metal and Hide—they don't have the mettle so they hide.

Congress authorized $3.1 million to convert a ferryboat in Baltimore into a crab restaurant.

Education Bored

It's not easy being in charge of education, but somebody's got to do it. Occasionally the issues are hot-ticket items best discussed behind closed doors. The California Board of Education decided to meet in secret to decide if it should meet in secret. That's right. No one was told what the second meeting would be about—it was secret. But according to law they have to announce if they are going to meet in secret—even if it's a secret. The law goes like this: Government Code Section 11126(q)2(a) ... "The California State Board of Education reserves the right to meet in closed session pursuant to Government Code Section 11126(q)2(a) to determine whether the facts or circumstances authorize it to meet in closed session pursuant to Government Code Section 11126(q)2(a)." I think if the Board of Education has something to say they should share it with the whole class.

"Students don't vote. Do you expect me to come in here and kiss your ass?"
—Senator Wyche Fowler (D-Georgia) in 1992, to young volunteers campaigning for deficit reductions. Fowler denied making the comment; the volunteers insisted he did.

Oil and Waterfowl Don't Mix

It was one of the worst environmental disasters of our time. On March 24, 1989, the oil tanker *Exxon Valdez* spilled thousands of gallons of oil off the shores of Alaska. Soon after this, some 36,000 dead birds were recovered from the waters; others washed up on shore, all covered in thick crude. Federal and state authorities thought the number of fatalities of our feathered friends was probably higher—and they set out to prove it. The U.S. Fish and Wildlife Service spent $600,000 for one study in which 219 birds were taken from remote locations, including national wildlife refuges, and killed. Their bodies were fitted with radio tracers, many were dipped in oil, and then they were thrown into the sea. Radio receivers picked up the signals from the dead birds and tracked their course in the ocean. The project was designed to demonstrate that thousands of other birds could have sunk to the ocean's floor, while others might have floated out to sea or washed up on deserted shores. Alaska's regional director of the Wilderness Society, Allen E. Smith, exclaimed, "I don't understand why they have to go out and kill a bunch of wildlife to prove what everybody already knows—that a bunch of wildlife was killed." Leave it up to the government to discover a way to kill two birds with one study.

In 1962 the Food and Drug Administration set out on a thirty-month program to review the harmful effects of nearly two hundred existing food-color additives. The thirty-month project was finally completed in 1990—twenty-eight years later.

A Platform with a Loose Plank

"I'm not going to come out with programs that will defeat me, no matter how I stand on that program, because I want to get elected. There may be some programs that you believe in and I believe in that will not be campaign issues, because if they are, I won't be governor."
—North Carolina Lieutenant Governor R. B. Jordan III, running for the Democratic gubernatorial nomination

In 1981 the Department of Agriculture decided that ketchup was a vegetable and could "be counted as one of the two vegetables required as part of the school lunch program."

All the News
That's Fit to Print

Pornography was rampant in Winchester, Indiana, so the fine folks on the city council decided to do something about it. They wrote a local antipornography ordinance to put a stop to smut. According to Indiana state law, any new ordinance must first be published in a local newspaper before it can become law. Unfortunately, the local newspaper thought the wording in the new ordinance was "obscene" and refused to print it.

"There are different Klans—just like there's different fraternities at a college."
—Louisiana's Republican Congressman David Duke explaining his former Ku Klux Klan membership

A Taxing Situation

Nobody likes to pay taxes—not even a city. The treasurer of Tulsa County in Oklahoma, unable to get the city to pay delinquent taxes on municipal property, demanded that eleven tracts of land be auctioned, including a twenty-four-acre strip of land purchased in 1985 for $1.5 million. The auction was a huge success, but not for the city; one lucky bidder got the $1.5 million tract of land for $200. That makes buying Manhattan Island from the Indians for a handful of beads look like a bum deal.

**"Hazards are one of the main
causes of accidents."**
*—From the U.S. Occupational Safety and Health
Administration's booklet "Safety with Beef Cattle," 1976*

How Do You Spell Relief?

Here's proof the United States Congress isn't full of hot air—it's full of gas. The U.S. government has 32 billion cubic feet of helium stored under twenty square miles of Texas Panhandle. Why? In case of blimp warfare. That's right, blimp warfare. And you thought the threat was nuclear war. Foolish citizen.

The National Helium Reserves was established by Congress in 1929 when blimps were thought to be the next phase in modern warfare. During the 1960s Congress decided to renew the reserves and ordered additions to the stockpile. In 1973 Congress finally realized we had enough helium and the chances of a blimp attack were dim, so they ordered the Bureau of Mines, which handles the program, to maintain the existing supply. They didn't get rid of it; they just stopped buying more. In 1993 the budget for this project was set at $22 million. Even though they plan to recoup this money by selling off small amounts of helium to other government agencies, their debt from buying and storing the helium now exceeds $1 billion, with annual interest payments of around $130 million. NASA and the Defense and Energy departments are their principal customers, and they're required by law to buy all their helium from the reserve, even though it costs more than helium from private suppliers. There goes our money—up, up, and away.

A bill was introduced into the Alaska legislature to punish "public flatulence, crepitation, gaseous emission, and miasmic effluence," carrying a penalty of $100.

The Proof Is in the Pudding

We've all heard the expression *a prostitute with a heart of gold,* but according to a proposed 1985 bill to legalize prostitution, this character trait would have to be proven when applying for a position as a prostitute. The Washington state bill would allow a person to hook "only upon satisfactory proof that the applicant is of good character." One can only imagine how applicants are to go about proving they are of good character.

"That's part of American greatness, is discrimination. Yes, sir. Inequality, I think, breeds freedom and gives a man opportunity."
—*Lester Maddox, former governor of Georgia (1966)*

The United States Pork Service, Uh, I Mean Park Service

There's more than just boring trees and squirrels in Pennsylvania state parks, thanks to two House representatives. There's also a string of Canadian steam locomotives and a series of rusty old buildings. Steamtown National Historic Site and America's Industrial Heritage Project are two examples of "park-barrel" politics.

Steamtown National Historic Site (aka Steamtown USA) was stoked by Joseph McDade (R-Pennsylvania). This sixty-two-acre project consists of a collection of Canadian steam locomotives and is considered by rail preservationists as a second-rate collection. There are at least four national railroad museums already, but McDade somehow hitched up his fellow congressmen to his project. McDade's engineering railroaded taxpayers into coughing up $65 million to build Steamtown, and $4 million per year for operations. At his last whistle-stop through Congress he got $11 million more for his ultimate train set. With all this money poured into Steamtown, how popular is it? Not very. Annual visits number around 130,000, compared to 4.8 million visitors at the Delaware Water Gap about an hour away.

America's Industrial Heritage Project was pieced together by Pennsylvania Democrat John Murtha and was approved by Congress in 1988. With a name like America's Industrial Heritage Project one would expect a glowing tribute to the men and women who shaped the economy and future of this great country of ours. Actually, it's a hodgepodge of rusty old factories, railroad artifacts (rejects from Steamtown, probably), and hiking trails, in southwestern Pennsylvania. Cost to taxpayers: over $60 million so far. There are Industrial Heritage Projects everywhere—but most of us call them inner cities.

The Illinois Department of Conservation spent $180,000 to study the contents of owl vomit.

A Rose by Any Other Name

Harry S Truman's middle name is "S"—there's no period; it's not an initial. His parents did this to appease both his grandfathers, whose names were Shippe and Solomon. There's another case of a person having only letters as his name—R B Jones. R B decided to enlist in the Army and to alleviate any problems with his name he courteously wrote it as "R(only) B(only) Jones." From that day on his dog tags, his assignment forms, and even his discharge papers were issued under the name "Ronly Bonly Jones."

$5 million was approved by Congress as an interest-free loan to Sears, Roebuck under the federal "antipoverty" funds program.

A Day Late and a Dollar Short

Wrapping up the end of a grueling 1988 campaign, Herbert Connolly, who was running to keep his seat on the Massachusetts governor's council, looked at his watch and realized he had to get to the polls before they closed. Unfortunately Connolly was fifteen minutes too late and wasn't allowed to vote. What's one vote? For Connolly, who's probably still kicking himself, it made all the difference. The final tally was 14,715 for Connolly and 14,716 for his opponent.

"Women prefer Democrats to men."
—*Representative Tony Coelho (D-California)*

Memories in the Making

Let's see what's developing in the criminal justice department. On January 15, 1992, Norman Parker, a supplies specialist with the United States Attorney's Office for the District of Columbia, pleaded guilty to charges of stealing from the government. Parker admitted to charging approximately $120,000 worth of Polaroid film to the United States Attorney's Office, then turning around and selling the film for personal profit. Say, "Cheese." He was sentenced to five years' probation and ordered to pay $10,000 in restitution. Also during his sentencing on March 12, 1992, because he "advanced the film," Parker was ordered to perform a hundred hours of community service.

In Acworth, Georgia, the city council passed an ordinance in 1982 requiring all households to own fishing poles.

Coffee, Tea, Parachute?

During the 1980s it was uncovered that the Air Force had paid $7,000 for the installation of a coffee machine. Why was the coffeemaker so expensive? It was guaranteed to survive a crash powerful enough to kill the entire crew. Good to the last drop!!!

"I wanted to have all my ducks in a row so if we did get into a posture we could pretty much slam-dunk this thing and put it to bed."

—Lee Cooke, *mayor of Austin, Texas*

Beating Welfare Is Hard Work

A lot of Americans can't understand why some welfare recipients don't get off the public dole and get a job. The answer is simple—jobs don't pay as well. The Cato Institute recently calculated the total value of all welfare-type benefits—from Medicaid, Aid to Families with Dependent Children, and Food Stamps, for recipients in all fifty states. It then took those tax-free incomes and compared them to the amount of money an equally paid worker would have left after taxes. Here are the results:

Welfare recipients in Alaska, Connecticut, the District of Columbia, Hawaii, Massachusetts, New York, and Rhode Island are given the equivalent of a twelve-dollar-per-hour job. Seventeen states provide welfare benefits worth at least ten dollars per hour (almost twice the federal minimum wage).

Forty-seven out of fifty states pay welfare benefits greater than the starting salary of a janitor. Twenty-nine states give out more than the average starting salary for a secretary, and nine, believe it or not, hand out taxpayer money that exceeds the typical first-year starting salary of a teacher. In Hawaii, in order to match the purchasing power of welfare benefits, a working mother with two children would have to earn $36,400. We're thinking of changing Uncle Sam's name to Daddy Warbucks.

"If anybody has any better ideas, I'm all ears."

—*Ross Perot, independent presidential candidate, 1992*

The More the Merrier

In March 1994 the Massachusetts Division of Medical Assistance announced it had spent nearly $50,000 on fertility drugs for 260 people. There's nothing really so bad about that until you learn that 80 of the recipients were welfare mothers, two of whom already had eight children each.

Richard T. Pisani, Democratic candidate for lieutenant governor in Missouri, officially changed his name to "Richard Thomas Bullet Train Pisani," to let voters know he was a proponent of the high-speed train.

The Disaster Masters

After public criticism for slow and uncoordinated action during Hurricane Andrew, which devastated parts of Florida, the Federal Emergency Management Agency (FEMA) knew exactly what it needed to do: spend $50,000 on billboards to improve its image and $73,000 on polo shirts for staff members. The agency also solicited bids for buttons and Frisbees imprinted with its 800 number. Rest assured that when the next disaster occurs, FEMA will be on the ball—and the Frisbees, and the buttons, and the billboards. . . .

"It's the responsibility of the media to look at the president with a microscope, but they go too far when they use a proctoscope."
—*Richard M. Nixon (Thirty-seventh President)*

Disorderly Conduct

We all agree that it's time to put criminals behind bars. But sometimes it's difficult to tell who the real criminals are. In fiscal year 1994 Congress appropriated $2,820,000 for a U.S. courthouse in Steubenville, Ohio. Sounds just like what we need—more courthouses to put away more crooks. But this project is continuing even though local judges admit an additional courthouse is unnecessary. In a letter to Congress, U.S. District Judge James Graham stated: "In my opinion, the construction of a courthouse in Steubenville and the creation of additional judgeships there would be a monumental waste of the taxpayers' money." The judge's concerns were overruled by Congress.

In June 1996 Scott Glasrud, an Albuquerque, New Mexico, schoolteacher, lost the Republican primary for a state senate seat by two votes. One month later he discovered that, because of a death in the family, his father-in-law and mother-in-law had failed to send in their write-in votes.

It Just Doesn't Add Up

With the taxpayers of the United States cowering at its very name, the Internal Revenue Service must be beyond reproach, right? They make all the tax codes, they've got the big computers, they have all the answers—unfortunately, half of their answers are wrong. According to a 1989 General Accounting Office (GAO) study of the accuracy of IRS answers to taxpayers inquiries, the IRS was two bricks shy of a load. Of 718 pieces of IRS correspondence, 31 percent had "critical errors," and 16 percent had additional errors that were "noncritical"—a failure rate of almost one in two! But even if their figures don't calculate, it's still your abacus on the line.

The Pentagon paid $1,676 for a ten-foot aluminum ladder.

Horning in on Nature

The United States government is the most powerful government on the face of the earth . . . so powerful, in fact, that it can redesign nature. What am I talking about? In 1983, five hundred deer crossing signs in Iowa showed deer silhouettes with a little Darwinian twist. Their antlers were on backward. An engineer for the Iowa Department of Transportation said the agency "just used the design that's in our manuals." I guess if you go by the strict code of law—it's okay in Iowa to hit a deer with its antlers on straight.

☆

$1 million added by the Senate to study brown tree snakes. The snake is found only in Guam, hasn't been proven to be life threatening to humans, and can't survive in North America. Makes you wonder who the real snakes are.

One for All and All for One

Tenses, Gender, and Number: For the purpose of the rules and regulations contained in this chapter, the present tense includes the past and future tenses, and the future, the present; the masculine gender includes the feminine, and the feminine, the masculine, and the singular includes the plural, and the plural the singular.

—Excerpt from the revised (1973) state code for the California Department of Consumer Affairs

$102,000 for a project by the National Institute on Alcohol Abuse and Alcoholism, including one experiment to see if sunfish that drink tequila are more aggressive than sunfish that drink gin.

More Precious than Gold

"Look, up in the air. It's a bird; it's a plane; no, it's a flying fortune." The B-2 bomber, at $2.2 billion per plane, is one of the most highly questioned purchases by the United States government in recent years. Let's do some math. An empty B-2 bomber weighs 160,000 pounds, which amounts to $15,714 per pound. A pound of pure twenty-four-carat gold (at $385 per troy ounce), on the other hand, is only $4,620. The craftsmanship on the B-2 bomber must be three times more precious than gold, right? Sorry. The B-2 was recently discovered to have radar that cannot distinguish between a rain cloud and a mountainside. But at least this fool's gold doesn't turn your finger green.

The Pentagon spends $8,612 per second, about $271.6 billion a year.

Smart Missiles?

In the middle of July there's no greater pleasure than relaxing at a summer cottage, dipping into the pool, or taking the boat for a spin around the lake. The most troubling aspects might be sunburn, mosquito bites, or getting bombed. I'm not talking about getting drunk, bombed, I'm talking literally being bombed. On July 18, 1994, Bob and Joan Hutton's summer cottage near Waters, Michigan, was accidentally bombarded by the Illinois National Guard. Fortunately, the couple was away at a screening of *Forest Gump*... and "Stupid is as stupid does," perfectly describes this explosive situation. A 105-millimeter howitzer shell blasted a three-foot-wide crater into the Huttons' yard, shattered several windows, and tore holes completely through the house. According to a Guard general, the missile "just barely went out of the buffer zone." Bob Hutton, while sifting through mounds of repair estimates, said, "The easiest thing now would probably be to sell the thing to the government for the end of their range. It'll give them a firing point or something."

$491,607 spent by the Department of Agriculture for a party in honor of nine hundred employees. How dare they spend that much, you say? The year before they spent $667,000.

Too Politically Correct

Sensitivity is running rampant in the United States. Every race, creed, nationality, sex, and national origin is devising a new name for itself. So, the government jumped on the bandwagon as well. When the county board of Walworth County, Wisconsin, drafted an antibigotry resolution in 1995, they felt they had to live up to the standards they were setting. In referring to white supremacist organizations, they changed the name "hate groups" to "unhappy groups."

"I didn't like it and I didn't inhale it."

—*1992 presidential candidate Bill Clinton, acknowledging that he "experimented once or twice" with marijuana in college*

That's 1-900-Sexy-IRS

Telephone directory assistance in Portland, Oregon, gave new meaning to the phrase *customer service*. In April 1995 the Internal Revenue Service's toll-free number was accidentally misprinted. Instead of hearing, "IRS, may I help you?" callers heard, "Hi, sexy," and were offered "phone phantasies" for up to $3.99 per minute. The calls weren't tax deductible, by the way.

"They're multipurpose. Not only do they put the clips on, but they take them off."
—Spokesman for defense contractor Pratt and Whitney in 1990, on why the company charged the Air Force $999.20 each for ordinary pliers. How could pliers cost so much? The contractor hired a subcontractor to build the pliers for a mere $669 each and then tacked on $330.20 each in overhead and profit.

"Ash Receivers, Tobacco (Desk Type)"

. . . That's how the government refers to a simple glass ashtray. The federal government has become so bloated that it takes weeks, months, and even years to buy items for its various departments. The General Services Administration (GSA) is responsible for buying all those little doodads that the government needs to exist. Like ashtrays. But they can't just be any run-of-the-mill ashtrays, they have to be government ashtrays; sorry, Government Ash Receivers, Tobacco (desk type). In March 1993, the GSA outlined, in nine pages of requirements, specifications, and drawings, the exact size, shape, color, style, function, and markings of a simple glass ashtray (read: Ash Receivers, Tobacco [desk type]) that would meet the rigorous government standards.

A Type I, square, glass, $4^{1}/_{2}$ inch (114.3 mm) ashtray (Ash Receivers, Tobacco [desk type]) must include the following features: "*A minimum of four cigarette rests, spaced equidistant around the periphery and aimed at the center of the receiver, molded into the top. The cigarette rests shall be sloped toward the center of the ash receiver. The rests shall be parallel to the outside top edge of the receiver or in each corner, at the manufacturer's option. All surfaces shall be smooth.*"

But what if the government gets a bad batch of ashtrays (Ash Receivers, Tobacco [desk types])? Never fear, trembling citizen, there are pages and pages of regulations to curtail such a horrible fate. The GSA requires that all ashtrays (you know what they're called) be tested in this way: "*The test shall be made by placing the specimen on its base upon a solid support (a 1 ^{3}/$_4$ inch, 44.5 mm maple plank), placing a steel center punch (point ground to a 60-degree included angle) in contact with the center of the inside surface of the bottom and striking with a hammer in successive blows of increasing severity until breakage occurs.*"

Is that it? Of course not, innocent taxpayer. Paragraph 4.5.2 states: "*The specimen should break into a small number of irregular-shaped pieces not greater in number than thirty-five, and it must not dice.*" Don't leave us hanging—what does *dice* mean? The paragraph goes on to explain: "*Any piece* ^{1}/$_4$ *inch (6.4 mm) or more on any three of its adjacent edges (excluding the thickness dimension) shall be included in the number counted. Smaller fragments shall not be counted.*"—Regulation AA-A-710E (superseding Regulation AA-A-710D)

The government has so many regulations that mistakes and overspending are impossible, right? If you believe that, you're nuts (Edible Dry Fruit, [Peanut Type]).

Undercover agents in Wisconsin once
used food stamps to buy a house.

Their Bark Is Worse than Their Bite

In 1994, Virginia Rugai (Nineteenth District, Chicago) proposed an ordinance that would fine dog owners $100 if their pets barked "for a period of five minutes or more without an interruption in excess of one minute." Although the ordinance had bite, it was quickly muzzled in committee.

In Clark County, Nevada, thirteen USDA employees from three different agencies serve forty farmers: that equals one bureaucrat for every three farmers.

The Three *R*'s: Reading, Writing, and Rufus

Remember the good old days of elementary-school math tests? "If a train left Detroit traveling fifty miles an hour . . ." et cetera? Now, in an age of exposing children to the "real world," comes the Charles Routen test. At Chicago's May Elementary School, public-school teacher Charles Routen administered a math test to his sixth-grade class in the spring of 1993. Here's one of the questions: "Rufus is pimping three girls. If the price is $65 for each trick, how many tricks will each girl have to turn so Rufus can pay for his $800-per-day crack habit?" After the test the teacher was asked a question: "How long will it take one rookie teacher to pack his bags and head out of town?" The answer? Not long—Routen resigned in late June 1994.

"When you get married you might expect you're going to get a little sex."

—*Senator Jeremiah Denton (R-Alabama), explaining why he's against rape legislation for victims within the marriage. Denton is best known as the Vietnam war hero who blinked out torture in Morse code when interviewed on TV.*

Car-Pay-Diem

In 1992 Judge George Best and U.S. Representative John Conyers, Jr. (D-Michigan) had finished campaigning at a Detroit community center when they realized both of their cars had been stolen. The vehicles were eventually recovered; but the tires, air bags, and other important parts had been stolen. What were the topics the judge and the congressman lectured on that fateful day in the community center in Detroit? Why, crime and safe streets, of course.

☆

"If I could be the condom queen **and get every young person in the United States who is engaging in sex to use a condom, I would wear a crown on my head with a condom on it."**
—*Surgeon General Joycelyn Elders in 1994*

Vive la Différence

In 1990 the Houston City Council wanted to crack down on indecent exposure. They were tired of seeing women's breasts, and by gosh they were going to do something about it. Their plan was to draft an ordinance outlawing women's bare breasts. In order to make sure the wording was beyond reproach, they hired a professional researcher. His job? To describe and detail why women's breasts are different from men's. Let's just hope it's not the same guy who wrote the dissertation on butts.

The Senate appropriated $200 million to buy 36 million pounds of depleted uranium, even though the government has a stockpile of depleted uranium to last for a hundred years—of war! The depleted uranium is being purchased from a company called Nuclear Metals, Inc., which produces it in South Carolina. Who put the item into the budget? South Carolina's Senator Strom Thurmond (Republican) and Senator Ernest Hollings (Democrat).

Coming Out of the Closet

There are no skeletons in South Dakota Senator Larry Pressler's closets—that's because he's in them most of the time. On one occasion Pressler took a nap in a closet, slept longer than he expected, and arrived late for an important hearing. Another day saw the Republican senator leave a meeting of the Commerce Committee and enter a closet believing it to be an exit. He was so embarrassed, he decided to stay in the closet until his fellow members left the room. This plan failed, however, when his colleagues decided to wait for him.

David Bonior (D-Michigan) got the Transportation Department to begin building a forty-mile, ten-foot-wide bike path through his own neighborhood.

Giving the Budget the Byrd

Here's a deal that would make Monty Hall proud. In 1989 the White House attempted to pass a supplemental budget that delivered aid to the contras in Nicaragua. Senator Robert Byrd (D-West Virginia) stonewalled signing the bill. He then casually mentioned that a government telescope in West Virginia had been blown down in a windstorm. Bush's budget director, Richard Darman, in the blink of an eye, quickly inserted a $75 million addition to the bill to replace Senator Byrd's telescope. Then and only then did Byrd sign the bill; which passed. Darman later told friends, "That was the cheapest $75 million telescope the federal government ever bought." Which just goes to prove, you don't always have to look into space to find a black hole.

$1 million to discover why people don't walk or ride bikes more often "as a means of transportation," sponsored by Representative Martin Olav Sabo (D-Minnesota).

A Road by Any Other Name

In 1995, just two years after Illinois House Republicans thwarted a proposal to name Interstate 57 after the late U.S. Supreme Court Justice Thurgood Marshall (they claimed new road signs would be too costly and a waste of taxpayers' money), GOP legislators proposed a bill to name the same highway after Ronald Reagan. It failed. Finally, justice served.

A survey by the Luntz Research Company in October 1995 showed that female baby-boomers and independents believe that Bob Barker, host of *The Price Is Right,* understands the value of a dollar more than their own congressperson.

Pension the Taxpayer's Assets

Of course we need to care for the men and women of the police force who walk the thin blue line. Too bad we couldn't have drawn a line through the amendment tacked on to a pension bill by Republican Assemblyman Roger P. McAuliffe of Chicago. The addition allows former police officers working as state representatives to continue collecting police pensions while, at the same time, earning pensions from the Assembly. Just for the record, the *only* person in the state who would benefit is—former police officer turned Republican assemblyman Roger P. McAuliffe. The *Chicago Sun-Times* dubbed the bill "The Roger P. McAuliffe Pension Beneficiary Amendment"; it was signed into law by Governor Edgar in July 1995. Roll over, Thomas Jefferson.

"Those who survived the San Francisco earthquake said, 'Thank God, I'm still alive.' But, of course, those who died, their lives will never be the same again."
—*Representative Barbara Boxer (D-California)*

The Great Grape Mystery

March 1989. The phone rings in the U.S. Embassy in Chile. It is an anonymous caller with a hot tip. Grapes headed to the U.S. have been injected with cyanide. The Food and Drug Administration quickly sets out on a mission to hunt down these Grapes of Wrath. In the blink of an eye the inspector finds three suspicious-looking grapes—they won't talk. These three grapes have a telltale ring of white powder on them; obviously he's found the right fruit. FDA experts know that harmful doses of cyanide make grapes shrivel and turn black, and cyanide would contaminate the entire batch. But these grapes are plump and healthy, and so is the rest of the batch. Could it have been a prank call? FDA Commissioner Frank Young thought not; he impounded the 2 million crates of grapes and sent out a warning to consumers not to eat Chilean fruit. Within weeks the Chilean private sector lost about $300 million and more than twenty thousand Chilean workers lost their jobs (and they don't have American-style unemployment insurance). It turned out that the 2 million crates of grapes were not contaminated; there was no cyanide. So what was the mysterious white powder? It was talc residue from sprays used by Chilean growers.

The Pentagon spends $119 million a year
for newspapers and periodicals.

Sprechen Sie Newt?

"You can now get a certificate to teach German by sitting through enough classes, but if you speak German, you can't teach German if you don't have a certificate. So you can have a German teacher who can't speak German, but though they have the certificate so they can teach, even though they can't teach.... If you can speak it, you can't teach it, even if you could teach it. Are you with me so far?"
—Speaker of the House, Newt Gingrich (R-Georgia); 1995

According to the Occupational Safety and Health Administration (OSHA), *sand,* including beach sand, is considered *poison* because it contains trace amounts of silica.

Free at Last,
Free at Last

On March 16, 1995, the Mississippi House of Representatives finally ratified the Thirteenth Amendment to the Constitution—abolishing slavery. The state didn't ratify the 1865 amendment earlier because legislators were angry they hadn't been reimbursed for the value of freed slaves. Why it took them over one hundred and thirty years to ratify the amendment nobody knows.

"It is about a socialist, antifamily political movement that encourages women to leave their husbands, kill their children, practice witchcraft, destroy capitalism, and become lesbians."

—Televangelist and 1988 GOP presidential candidate Pat Robertson, in 1992, on the proposed Equal Rights Amendment

Highest on the Hog

The 1996 Congressional Pig Book Summary issued by the Citizens Against Government Waste awarded Senator Daniel Inouye (D-Hawaii) the "Oinkers" Lifetime Achievement Award. Senator Inouye used his power in Congress to send a total of $67 million in "pork" projects to his home state in 1996; making a grand total of $609,995,000 since 1991! With that much pork he'd be able to throw a luau for the whole world.

In 1995 the Tennessee Department of Environment and Conservation investigated the trail of a container leaking radioactive material—the container was purchased at a yard sale.

Insufficient Postage

Here's something to write home about. In May 1994 postal executive Celestine Green was given a $60,000 remodeling budget to spruce up her office, and she spent it all on new furniture, fixtures, and doodads. But she neglected to account for installation charges, and when she received the bill there was more to the price than postage due. The installation fees pushed the price to almost $200,000. According to Ms. Green, she didn't realize she would be charged for the installation; she assumed postal workers would do it for free. The final stamp of stupidity is that the building that held Green's office was in the process of being abandoned for new quarters when the remodeling was done.

P.S. Green has been rerouted to a lesser Postal Service position in suburban Bedford Park, Illinois.

$57,000 spent by the Executive Branch for gold-embossed playing cards to be used aboard Air Force Two.

Disabling the Entrepreneur

Blair Taylor was excited about his new business, a restaurant in Denver, Colorado, called the Barolo Grill. In December 1992, just a few days after his restaurant's grand opening, Taylor received a phone call from the U.S. Justice Department. "We have a complaint that your restaurant is in noncompliance with the Americans with Disabilities Act," said a Civil Rights Division attorney. The forty-year-old Taylor had not received any complaints and had no idea what complying with the Americans with Disabilities Act encompassed. The Americans with Disabilities Act (ADA) was enacted by Congress in 1990, to guarantee access to public facilities for people with disabilities. One provision required any public facility under construction or renovation "make alterations in such a manner that, to the maximum extent feasible, the altered portions are readily accessible to and usable by individuals with disabilities."

The U.S. Justice Department charged Taylor of situating eight of the restaurant's twenty-four tables on an eighteen-inch elevated platform without building a wheelchair ramp. On top of that, Taylor had not constructed a ramp from the sidewalk to the front of his building and up the seven-inch step to the doorway. He explained to the agency that sixteen of his tables were still wheelchair accessible and that two valet attendants were stationed in front of the restaurant to help customers through the entrance. To Justice Department attorney Bebe Novich that wasn't good enough. Taylor agreed to build a new ramp in the spring because it was too cold in December for concrete to set properly.

Months later, on April 9, a van pulled up and twenty protesters, ten of them in wheelchairs, staged an impromptu demonstration in front of Taylor's restaurant. Not only did they carry signs that read DOWN ON BAROLO and BLAIR SUCKS, they had a photographer accompany them who happily took pictures of the wheelchair-bound protesters as they blocked the front entrance to Taylor's restaurant. From the back, one protester shouted, "You promised Bebe Novich you would get us a ramp!" Since this information came from a private phone call with the Justice Department, Taylor believed from that comment that the protest had been arranged with the Justice Department's knowledge.

Not wanting to lose any more business, Taylor constructed the wheelchair ramp himself. He did this without securing city building permits, since the approval process would have taken up to four months. He had blueprints drawn up for the interior ramp and bathrooms that would meet all ADA specifications.

But in June, Taylor got hit from the other side. The city building inspector ruled the Barolo Grill had to obtain permits, not just for the areas to be renovated, but for the entire structure. The inspector then slapped a cease-and-desist order on Taylor, forbidding him from any ADA-mandated work until the local permits were issued.

After months of hearings before city officials and zoning boards, Taylor finally received his permits, in February 1994. He informed the Justice Department of the nature of his delay in meeting their mandates and they in turn threatened him with a lawsuit for non-compliance. Eager to get the government off his back and go about business as usually, Taylor began construction of handrails on the front entrance ramp, reconstructing wheelchair-friendly bathrooms, adding strobe-light fire alarms for the hearing impaired, and adding an interior ramp. He completed the final construction on April 1. But, April fools, the government still wasn't happy. On April 11, as he awaited customers by his new front entrance ramp, he was slapped with a federal lawsuit on the grounds of noncompliance with the ADA. What was it this time? The lawsuit demanded that Taylor rebuild the entire front ramp again because its handrail was not precisely 1 1/2 inches from the window glass. It was off by two inches. He was to redo the interior ramp, move the bathroom walls three inches closer to the toilets, install signs identifying bathrooms and exits in Braille, and even make a wine-storage room wheelchair accessible.

Taylor finally settled the case in November 1994 and agreed to take all steps necessary to fulfill the Justice Department's demands. He had menus printed in Braille, he produced an employee manual on serving to the disabled, and even sponsored a one-day "ADA awareness seminar" for restaurant owners in the Denver area. He had to make further construction designs on the building and was forced to pay four of the wheelchair protesters $1,500 each for the "humiliation" they had suffered while picketing his restaurant. The entire process took nearly two years to complete and cost

Taylor an estimated $100,000 in legal bills, fines, and construction. Now the question isn't the one Taylor asked—"Why me?"—the real question is how many wheelchair-bound customers Taylor has had in his restaurant since the construction?

"Oh, that was just an accident that happened."
—*President Nixon, on why there was a mysterious eighteen-minute silence on one of the key Watergate tapes*

Getting Testy

This is a test—this is only a test. Here's a sample from a question-naire compiled and funded by the Federal Highway Administration (FHA) in the late 1970s.

Do you consider that large trucks:

    a) contribute to traffic congestion?
    b) block a driver's vision?
    c) travel too fast on highways?
    d) travel too slow going up hills?
    e) make a side splash on wet roads that is a problem?
    f) make smoke and fumes that might be a problem?

Here's another question for you:
How much do you think was spent on research for this test?

    a) $2,000
    b) $15,000
    c) $222,000
    d) $175,000

The answer is (c)—$222,000.

The bigger question is . . . why?

"Located profitable areas for the concentration of resources."

—*Pentagon term for* bombing

Old Glory and a Matching Handkerchief

In August 1994 the Republican political caucus in Grand Rapids, Michigan, was about to get under way. The coffee and cookies were gone, the handshaking and backslapping was over, and it was time to get down to business. But there was a problem—no one had brought an American flag . . . and since the beginning of each meeting starts with the Pledge of Allegiance, the caucus would be detained. But quick-thinking party member Jack Pettit had a solution. He stood on a chair in front of the crowd and displayed his tie, which had a stars-and-stripes motif. The other members solemnly placed their hands over their hearts, recited the pledge, and began their meeting.

"One word sums up probably the responsibility of any vice president, and that one word is *to be prepared*."
—*Vice President Dan Quayle*

It's Not My Job

The United States Government's Food and Drug Administration takes longer to approve or disapprove drugs than similar agencies in any other country in the world. It's great to think they're being cautious; but maybe there's another reason. The FDA recently put out their *Equal Employment Opportunity Handbook* spelling out "practical" guidelines for hiring. One segment of the handbook related this hiring tidbit: The normal requirement for "knowledge of rules of grammar" and "ability to spell accurately" should be overlooked, since it may interfere with hiring of "underrepresented groups or individuals with disabilities." The statute later explains that the interview process should not be used "to judge highly subjective traits such as motivation, ambition, maturity, personality, and neatness." If these rules were in effect in 1776 the Declaration of Independence might have read: *Wee wholed thees truffs tobe celf evedant? that al men r creeted =.*

Hillary Clinton often ends conversations with staff members with "Okey-dokey, artichokey."

Bladder Control to Major Tom

The life of a jet pilot may seem to be a glamorous one: cool leather jacket, shiny helmet, Tom Cruise haircut. But it's not always what it seems. Take, for instance, Lieutenant Colonel Don Snelgrove. In October 1993 Snelgrove set his F-16C fighter jet on automatic pilot while he did a decidedly unglamorous task—go to the bathroom. While trying to get to his "piddle pack," a plastic bag containing a dehydrated sponge, Snelgrove got into a jam. His belt's buckle became wedged between the control stick and the ejection seat. When he tried to adjust the seat, the control stick slammed to the right, causing the F-16C to plummet from 33,000 feet to 2,000 feet. At this rate of descent it was impossible for Snelgrove to regain control of his jet. He ejected, and the $18 million fighter jet disintegrated on impact somewhere in Turkey. This whole ordeal would never have happened if Lieutenant Colonel Snelgrove had heeded some motherly advice—"I told you to go before we left home!"

☆

Representative George Beard of
**Culpepper, Virginia, proposed a bill
to the statehouse which prohibited
dead bodies from being stored
where food is served.**

Jail Bait

The trap was set. The Wildlife Division of Ohio had been hot on the heels of a notorious dealer. Fourteen agents and two undercover agents had spent three harrowing weeks on the job. Surveillance was around the clock. Photographs were taken from the safety of surrounding bushes. Brave agents even made purchases to make sure they had the right man. Over $25,000 in wages was spent on one suspected criminal. Who was this danger to the citizens of Ohio? He was an eight-year-old boy who had been selling worms from a makeshift stand in front of his parents' house. Surveillance proved that, other than the occasional buy from undercover operatives, the boy sold worms to only four passing fishermen. The case was dismissed and the boy and the worms were let off the hook.

"It sucked!"
—Tennessee Republican congressional candidate Steve Gill, on how it felt to lose to Bart Gordon in the 1994 election

And Never the Train Shall Meet

June 13, 1994, was a day of celebration. Distinguished guests and dignitaries gathered in Wilmette, Illinois, to witness the ribbon-cutting ceremony for a new maintenance shop for Chicago Transit Authority (CTA) trains. People realized something was a little off track as the first car rumbled toward the shop at the end of the Evanston line—the door was about a foot too low for the train to enter; or the train was about a foot too high, depending on how you look at it. "However you phrase it," explained one CTA official, "somebody goofed." CTA spokesman Jeff Stern promised the city would not be responsible for the repair, while at the same time, Schwendener construction is seeking $20,000 reimbursement from the CTA for raising the opening. James Arnold, executive vice-president of Schwendener Construction, made it clear his contractors built the shop according to the CTA architect's design.

"I don't know every damned thing in that ethics law."
—*South Carolina State Senator Robert Ford, in May 1994, after it was revealed that he used taxpayers' money to mail advertisements for his Charleston car dealership*

One from Column "A" and One from Column "B"

Double dipping isn't a term for ice cream hogs—it's a term for money hogs. Take, for example, former state senator John Orabona of Providence, Rhode Island. Retired in 1995, Orabona is now seeking pension credit for seventy-nine years of state and city employment—but he's only fifty-two years old. How can a former school administrator, mayoral aide, and schoolteacher be so terrible at math? It's all in the numbers. We can trace Orabona's claim of longevity to payments he made to both the city and the state pension plan for the same years of employment—"double dipping." Orabona is seeking a total of $106,000 in pension per year, nearly $30,000 a year more than the highest salary he ever received from the city or the state. It has also come to light that Orabona, during his term, voted on several pieces of legislation that increased his pension. Don't despair, there was a special pop quiz for Orabona—the State Ethics Commission investigated his mathematical skills, but no charges have been filed yet.

The Bureau of Indian Affairs included in their 1992 inventory list: $297 million for three chain saws ($99 million each), one television set at $96 million, and two typewriters—one at $77 million and a cheaper model at $42 million.

Frankly, My Deer, I Don't Give a Damn

It's a quiet, dark Iowa night and you're driving down a back road; windows down, radio turned up. Suddenly, there is a loud thump, you lose control of your steering wheel, and swerve over to the side of the road. You've struck a deer. Your car is wrecked. What can you do? What *can* you do? Never fear—Representative Jim Meyer, second-term Republican from Iowa, is here. In early 1996, Meyer proposed a bill that would pay motorists $100 if they struck a deer. In the "Bambi Bill," which some legislators consider "one of the dumbest pieces of legislation in history," accidental trophy hunters would receive payment from the Department of Natural Resources (DRN) trust fund, which traditionally funds land conservation efforts.

According to Meyer, Iowa has a deer problem the DRN can't seem to control. "This isn't a car problem. It's a deer problem," said Meyer. "I feel sorry for the people who are driving down the road and run into a deer. They're inconvenienced. Their car's wrecked." Meyer, a former farmer, who admitted to stirring five-gallon buckets of the toxic herbicide atrazine with his bare hands ("I did that for years. It never hurt me") did allow that "turkeys can sometimes make an awful mess," but this bill applies only to deer. Dough for Doe—what will they think of next?

In 1986 the National Park Service purchased a half acre of land in southwest Washington, D.C., for $230,000. In 1988 it was discovered that the Park Service already owned the land—they bought it in 1914.

Come Listen to My Story 'bout a Lady Named Kulp

You can still see her in reruns of *The Beverly Hillbillies*. Nancy Kulp played Jane Hathaway, the long-faced secretary to Milburn Drysdale, for nine seasons. But here's something you probably didn't know. She ran for U.S. Congress from the state of Virginia in 1984. Kulp, who worked for Adlai Stevenson in his failed 1952 presidential race against Eisenhower, also worked with the Democratic State Committee of Pennsylvania and was elected to the Board of Directors of the Screen Actors Guild in 1982. She ran unopposed in the Democratic congressional primary and got the nod as the Democratic nominee. But during her campaign against opponent Bud Shuster, she heard a familiar voice on the radio. Buddy Ebsen, who played Jed Clampett, taped a radio commercial for Kulp's opponent, which said: "I dropped [Nancy] a note to say, 'Hey, Nancy, I love you dearly but you're too liberal for me—I've got to go with Bud Shuster." After the race, Nancy probably felt like loading up her truck and moving to Beverly . . . Hills, that is. She lost the race 117,203 to 59,449.

The Environmental Protection Agency gave Rolex watches to employees of their contractors.

"I have opinions of my own—strong opinions—but I don't always agree with them."

—*George Bush (Forty-first President)*

To OSHA a Hero Is Just a Sandwich

Twenty-one-year-old Dwight Kaufman was working in a dirt trench at a construction site near Boise, Idaho, when the wall collapsed and buried him alive. Thankfully, Kevin Gill and another employee of DeBest Plumbing, Inc., Myron Jones, were there and quickly jumped into action. With time running out the two men dug at the dirt with their bare hands, removing enough dirt to expose Kaufman's head and allowing him to breathe. "We could hear muffled screams. You could just see about one inch of the back of his head," Gill said. "His shoulders were pinned from the collapsed piece. With his head covered, I think he would have died." Moments later a rescue team arrived and pulled Kaufman from his dirt grave. The two Samaritans didn't expect anything for their heroic deed, but they got something from the government anyway. They got fined. The Occupational Safety and Health Administration slapped a $7,875 penalty on the Boise plumbing company because the workers didn't put on hard hats and took no precautions against further cave-ins during their rescue. "Rescues must only be attempted after taking proper precautions to ensure that victims and would-be rescuers are not injured in secondary cave-ins," said Idaho OSHA Director Ryan Kuemichel. After hearing about the preposterous fine, Senator Dirk Kempthorne (R-Idaho) requested the Labor Department review the case. They did, and the fines were dropped.

"Thank goodness there are still people in this world who are willing to help their neighbor—despite an absurd bureaucratic mindset in the federal government that would seem to discourage saving a life," remarked Kempthorne. The senator is drafting legislation that will exempt acts of heroism from OSHA fines. Dwight Kaufman should be thankful—if he fell into the bottomless pit of OSHA regulations, he would have never climbed out.

The United States Supreme Court once ruled federal income tax unconstitutional—until the Sixteenth Amendment to the Constitution was ratified on February 3, 1913.

A Byrd in the Hand Is Worth Two in the Bush

Having a building named after you has got to be one of the greatest honors imaginable. So if you visit West Virginia, home of Democratic Senator Robert C. Byrd, you'll discover the most honored man in history—a legend in his own mind. Bearing his name are the: Robert C. Byrd Expressway, Robert C. Byrd Highway, Robert C. Byrd Industrial Park, Robert C. Byrd High School, Robert C. Byrd Aerospace Technology Center, Robert C. Byrd Bridge, Robert C. Byrd Institute for Advanced Flexible Manufacturing, Robert C. Byrd Visitors Center at Harpers Ferry National Historical Park, Robert C. Byrd Hardwood Technology Center, Robert C. Byrd Cancer Research Center, Robert C. Byrd Locks and Dam, Robert C. Byrd Institute, Robert C. Byrd Health Sciences Center of West Virginia University, Robert C. Byrd Community Center, Robert C. Byrd Honors Scholarships, and the Robert C. Byrd Scholastic Recognition Award. And the winner of this year's Robert C. Byrd Recognition Award is . . . May I have the envelope, please? Robert C. Byrd. What a surprise!

"The people of West Virginia don't need a lobbyist. They have me."
—*Robert C. Byrd (D-West Virginia)*

A Case of the Occult

In 1992 the Texas Alcoholic Beverage Commission temporarily prohibited the sale and distribution of Dixie Blackened Voodoo lager beer, not because there were product violations, but because the commission feared the name would encourage witchcraft, voodoo, and other occult practices. It's a wonder they haven't outlawed Black Magic Markers.

In 1920 Socialist and presidential candidate Eugene Debs received 920,000 votes even though he ran his entire campaign while in jail.

Cold Cash

The best state in which to live high on the hog, or high on the "pork," is North Dakota. Because of the wheat, which is subsidized, and the missiles the Pentagon stores there, which are subsidized, plus countless, but questionable, highway crossings, dams, and research grants to study such things as wheat weevils, North Dakotans pay a total of about $2 billion in federal taxes but get close to $3 billion in federal spending.

"I never said I had no idea about most of the things you said I said I had no idea about."

—*Assistant Secretary of State Elliott Abrams about his involvement in the 1987 Iran-Contra scandal*

The Devil and Webster's Dictionary

Remember in school if you didn't know how to spell a word the teacher told you to look it up? But how could you look it up if you didn't know how to spell it? Well, the United States government took that age-old question one step further. In the late 1970s the Smithsonian Institution spent nearly $89,000 to have a dictionary produced, edited, and printed in Tzotzil, an unwritten and obscure Mayan language, spoken by only 120,000 corn farmers in southern Mexico, who also speak Spanish. It's even more difficult to find this dictionary's meaning because it's written only in the specific dialect of Tzotzil spoken by about one twelfth, or ten thousand, members of this Mexican group of Mayan descent. Here's the clincher: There are no Spanish or English translations or definitions in the dictionary—so unless you already know how to speak Tzotzil, you're out of luck. Even the author of the dictionary admits, in his introduction, that this volume isn't particularly in demand, even in southern Mexico. How do you spell *waste*? Look it up!

The ratio of educational funding: Special
education programs: eleven dollars.
Gifted children: one cent.

The Ties Have It

Returning the reins of government to the people was what the Waco, Texas, city council had in mind. They voted on the time of day their council meetings should begin; the vote was a tie. One ingenious member thought the public should vote on this hotly contested issue. But before they could allow the people to vote, they had to vote to see if they were in agreement. They voted. The result? A three-to-three tie.

$161,913 spent by the National Institutes of Health to study "Israeli Reactions to SCUD Attacks During the Gulf War." (Result: It bothered them.)

You Won't Qualify Unless You Don't Qualify

We've all heard of people not getting jobs because they are "overqualified," but you never hear about underqualified people getting jobs—unless you've applied at the U.S. Forest Service. The Forest Service has been repeatedly criticized in the past for not hiring enough female firefighters. In many cases women were denied jobs because they were unable to pass the rigorous strength test required for hauling heavy firefighting equipment. In order to get the critics off their back the Forest Service decided to modify their position announcements. So they released an announcement that read, "Only unqualified applicants may apply." Another one specified, "Only applicants who *do not* meet [job requirement] standards will be considered." I'm not drawing any conclusions, but haven't there been a lot of forest fires lately?

During an interview at a Boise, Idaho, television station in April 1996, anesthesiologist William Levinger, running for the Republican senatorial nomination, began taking off his clothes, then propositioned a reporter, offering $5,000 for a kiss. Levinger checked into a mental health unit but still won 32 percent of the vote.

Endangered or in Danger

I smell a rat could be the slogan for twenty-nine homeowners when fire ravaged their property in Riverside County, California, in October 1993. An estimated $1 billion in property was lost thanks to the Stephens' kangaroo rat and the Endangered Species Act. In September 1988 the Stephens' kangaroo rat was officially placed on the list of endangered species. In order to protect its natural environment the government set aside 500,000 acres, 50,000 of which were "off limits" to humans. In 1992, before the beginning of the fire season, the Riverside County Fire Department ordered local residents to clear the dangerous and highly flammable brush that grew around their property as a preventative measure—but the Fish and Wildlife Service (FWS) said, "No!" They feared that destroying the growth would cause the little furry ones undue stress. Less than a year later, most people watched in amazement and disbelief as their homes, not to mention the homes of the Stephens' kangaroo rat, were engulfed by flames. One treasonous homeowner, thinking to himself, *What am I? A man or a mouse?* defied the FWS directive, jumped on his tractor, and quickly cleared a large tract of land, successfully saving his home from the fire. That same week in Orange and San Diego counties, hundreds lost their homes because they had the misfortune to live in the same federally protected, and highly flammable, area as another endangered species, the gnatcatcher. It seems like most times when an endangered species lives in the same area you do—well, there goes the neighborhood.

Each senator has forty aides, not counting those on his/her committees.

Computer Error

These days computers are essential for handling the daily input and output of government. Judith Kraines, county controller in Reading, Pennsylvania, voiced her department's computer problem at the January 1996 meeting of county commissioners. The problem was not that she didn't have a computer—but that her computer hadn't worked in two years. She was forced to type letters, memos, and do all written business on a typewriter. "If we had a computer," she stated, "letters would go out faster." Three days after the meeting, Kraines announced the computer she'd been complaining about had been fixed. The problem that had eluded her for two years? It wasn't plugged in.

$107,000 was appropriated by Congress for a project to study the sex life of the Japanese quail.

The Wall of Shame

The press was there. The crowd was there. The chairman was there. July 1993 was groundbreaking time for the town-house project at 1500 North Clybourn Avenue in Chicago. This was the beginning of a new era in low-income housing—the redevelopment of Cabrini Green, the notorious "projects" of *Good Times* fame. Chicago Housing Authority (CHA) chairman Vince Lane was to swing a ceremonial sledgehammer into the old building on the site. One problem: the demolition crew had prematurely leveled the building, leaving nothing for the chairman to whack. Quick as ants the CHA tailor-made a wall for Lane to knock down. Donning goggles, a hard hat, and a smile that would bring tears to your eyes, Lane knocked down the new taxpayer-built wall, and thus laid the groundwork for the future of low-income housing.

"Power-mongering men with short penises."
—*California State Assembly Speaker Doris Allen's opinion, shortly before her resignation, of her critics*

The Flames of Desire

In 1990 Hightstown, New Jersey, was a small metropolis of about 5,100 residents. But even in a small town bureaucrats will be bureaucrats; and they decided it was high time that Hightstown joined the big league. These safety-conscious officials deemed it necessary for their little three-stoplight town to buy a state-of-the-art fire truck with a retractable ladder that would extend 135 feet into the air. That way, they concluded, their town would be safe from the type of fires that had destroyed such cities as Chicago. In order to get this fire truck, city officials had to cough up over a half a million dollars from the city treasury. But that didn't deter the leaders of Hightstown. Soon the bright-red fire truck was seen in local parades and lovingly washed by the all-volunteer fire department. The 135-foot ladder was never used to put out any towering infernos, however. Why? Because the tallest building in Hightstown (excluding water towers and church steeples) is only 40 feet high.

Congress approved $1 million to be
spent in Trenton, New Jersey, to
preserve a sewer as a historic
monument. The brick-lined sewer is
twenty-five feet underground and has
been visited by only two people in the
past twenty-three years.

It's a Bird.
It's a Plane.
It's . . . Superfund!

If the federal government could figure out how to double its money like it has doubled toxic waste, we could balance the federal budget in a week. The Environmental Protection Agency's cleanup of the Vertac toxic waste site in Jacksonville, Arkansas, was an example of the Superfund in action. Superfund! Slower than a lame turtle, more powerless than a malnourished kitten, able to waste billions in a single bound. Superfund is the EPA's toxic waste cleanup program. Sounds great. But of the projected $13.5 billion spent since its creation in 1980, 25 percent of the money has gone to pay lawyers and consultants. So what about the other 75 percent? Has it saved lives? "The best estimate for the number of people who die each year from exposure to chemicals in Superfund sites is zero," according to the American Council of Science and Health.

Here's the Vertac story. In the mid-1980s the governor of Arkansas, Bill Clinton, authorized the EPA to incinerate dioxin at Vertac. Unfortunately there were no incinerators that could meet the federal standard for burning dioxin (requiring 99.9999 percent be destroyed). The dioxin had to be mixed with other materials before it could be incinerated, thereby producing two barrels of ash for every barrel of dioxin. The old fishes-and-loaves story with a horrible twist. The EPA then spent $300,000 for special storage buildings to house the dioxin ash. Why not simply store the dioxin in the storage buildings? Another burning question.

Among five hundred entries in the "Name the Army Material Command Building" contest, the winning entry was "The AMC Building."

The Sorcerer's Amendment

When someone commits a horrendous or unnatural crime, the defense will try to claim insanity. New Mexico's Republican State Senator Duncan Scott got tired of these "crazy" pleas and the psychologists and psychiatrists who testify in their favor. In 1995 he proposed an amendment that would draw attention to the rise of "insanity pleas in criminal trials," and put these "wizards of weirdness" into their proper outfit.

> When a psychologist or psychiatrist testifies during a defendant's competency hearing, the psychologist or psychiatrist shall wear a cone-shaped hat that is not less than two feet tall. The surface of the hat shall be imprinted with stars and lightning bolts.
>
> Additionally, the psychologist or psychiatrist shall be required to don a white beard that is not less than eighteen inches in length, and shall punctuate crucial elements in his testimony by stabbing the air with a wand.
>
> Whenever a psychologist or psychiatrist provides expert testimony regarding the defendant's testimony, the bailiff shall dim the courtroom lights and administer two strikes to a Chinese gong.

The amendment was approved by the state senate but rejected by the New Mexico House of Representatives, which begs the question, "How does that make you feel?"

"You will find it a distinct help . . . if you know and look as if you know what you are doing."

—*IRS training manual*

Don't Leave Home Without It

During the World Cup soccer competition Addison, Texas, city officials warned restaurant owners to be wary of possible credit-card fraud perpetrated by Nigerians who came to support their soccer team. Councilman Dick Wilke said restaurant owners should inform the police "if thirty people come in speaking Nigerian." There's only one problem with this level of alertness—there is no such language as Nigerian; the country's official language is English.

"Weather's like rape—long as it's inevitable, you might as well lie back and enjoy it."
—Clayton Williams, Republican gubernatorial candidate of Texas

I'm Going to Disney World

It was a real political party!!! The National Conference of State Legislators brought 1,700 legislators from all fifty states, their spouses, and children, to a conference at Florida's Disney World. You think that's goofy? The taxpayers picked up the $3 million tab.

"You hear about constitutional rights, free speech, and the free press. Every time I hear these words I say to myself, 'That man is a Red, that man is a Communist!' You never hear a real American talk like that."
—*Mayor Frank Hague, Jersey City, New Jersey, 1938*

There's a Hole in Washington Where All the Money Goes

What a wonderful world it would be if we could all give ourselves automatic pay raises, new furniture, or a private subway. But this is America—people have to pay for their own possessions, right? Not if you're America's privileged class—Congress. Here are just a few items Congress have contributed to themselves in the early 1990s; thanks to our tax money.

> *$8 million for new Senate elevators;*
> *$6 million to refurbish the Senate's private subway;*
> *$2 million to upgrade a House restaurant;*
> *$375,000 to renovate the House beauty parlor;*
> *$250,000 to study placement of television lights in the Senate;*
> *$40,000 for new wastebaskets; and*
> *$25,000 to study the best location for a new House gym.*

Our thank-you notes must have gotten lost in the mail.

The EPA launched a study in 1993 into the dangers of breathing while you take a shower—specifically, whether one might be injured by inhaling water vapor.

Catch-22

"This is another fine mess you've gotten me into" could be said by the people of Borneo when the World Health Organization tried to help them with their mosquito problem in the 1960s. First the World Health Organization sponsored a program to kill mosquitoes by using U.S.-made DDT. Everything seemed great for a while, but the powerful chemical disrupted the food chain and soon the entire island was overrun with rats. What was the U.S.'s solution to deal with the rats? They parachuted in hundreds of cats.

☆

$5 million approved by the Senate to renovate buildings and finish an aircraft hangar at Michigan's Wurtswirth Air Force Base—after the decision was made to close the base.

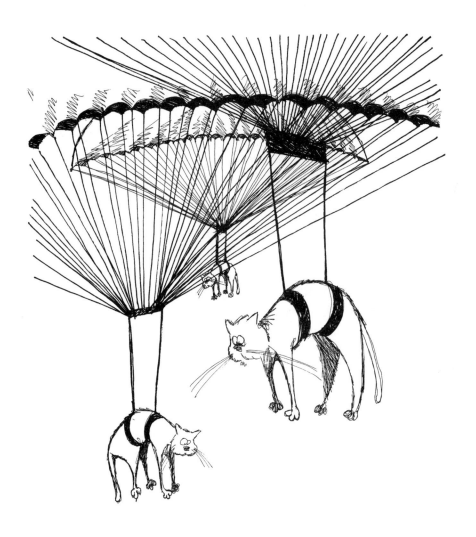

Dammed If You Do— Dammed If You Don't

What happens when the government gives a dam? In one case—disaster. In June of 1976 Idaho's federally constructed Teton Dam collapsed, completely destroying the small town of Wilford and devastating Idaho Falls. Eleven people died in the ensuing flood—and thousands more would have perished had the dam burst at night. When the dam site was given the okay, the bureaucrats should have put their finger in the dike (where they had their finger at this time no one is sure). It turns out that the Teton Dam was built in a seismic ashflow region; basically, the most unstable ground imaginable. As one geologist put it, "It was such an obviously lousy site to a trained geologist, it makes you wonder what happens to human judgment inside a bureaucracy." The Teton Dam cost taxpayers $85 million to build. The damage caused by the decision to build it cost taxpayers around $2 billion, plus the lives of eleven people.

You'd think the water supplied by the Teton Dam was desperately needed. But no. Of the eleven thousand previously cultivated acres planned to receive water from the project, average yearly irrigation was at 132 inches—an amount normally attributed to a tropical forest. This dam supplied a few farmers with an extra five inches of water a year. So in essence, the Bureau of Reclamation was, at a huge expense to taxpayers, giving water to extraordinarily water-wealthy farmers. Six months later the Idaho Water Users' Association, adding insult to ignorance, called for a "safe" Teton dam—to be built on the same site! Fortunately, that recommendation went down the drain.

$84,000 approved by Congress for a project to discover why people fall in love.

Washington Waste—
Batteries Not Included

In 1996, $15 million in taxpayer money was appropriated by the Senate and channeled through the Department of Defense for electric-vehicle research, in spite of continuing and extensive private-sector efforts. In 1995, $30 million was added and in 1994, Congress provided $45 million for research and development of electric vehicles: bringing the total in the last three years to a whopping $90 million—and how many electric vehicles have you seen on the streets?

Twenty-one congressmen, their spouses, staff, and guests—more than a hundred people—went to the Paris Air Show courtesy of the taxpayer. Cost? Over $200,000.

Farming Out the Money

Farmers have the greatest bank in the world—the United States government. According to the General Accounting Office, borrowers who have previously reneged on their direct or guaranteed loans are eligible to receive new guaranteed loans through the Farmers Home Administration (FmHA). During fiscal year 1991–1993, FmHA made approximately $55 million in new direct loans to 936 borrowers after it had been kind and good-hearted enough to forgive about $133 million on their previous direct loans. FmHA administers the federal government's largest direct lending program under the Consolidated Farm and Rural Development Act, aptly abbreviated as the "Con Act." And I remember getting a service charge from my bank when I was twelve cents shy on my account—where's my hoe?

"We don't necessarily discriminate. We simply exclude certain types of people."
—*Lieutenant Colonel Gerald Wellman, defending the military ban on gays*

Merry XXXmas

Christmas is the busiest time of the year for the post office. People mail millions of boxes, cards, and letters to friends and relatives everywhere in the world. It's a happy time, a joyous time. So it came as some surprise to the good people of Ohio when twelve thousand pieces of mail were stamped with an unusual greeting of holiday cheer. Instead of a brightly stamped "MERRY CHRISTMAS," the Yuletide mail recipients got a Scroogy "YOU BITCH" stamped on their mail, courtesy of their local post office. It gives the expression *Ho, ho, ho* a whole new meaning.

"Funds obligated for military assistance
as of September 3, 1979, may, if
deobligated, be reobligated."
—*Budget of the United States, fiscal 1980*

The Tales of Yellowtail

During the final three weeks of the 1996 Democratic congressional primary in Montana, Bill Yellowtail, a former state senator and EPA administrator, admitted that: 1) as a student at Dartmouth he was expelled for trying to break in to the same camera store . . . twice; 2) he once slapped his wife with so much force, she was admitted to a hospital; and 3) there was a lien on his Senate paycheck for failing to pay child support. Yellowtail gave the voters the old one, two, three, and still won the election.

In April 1993 the Montana legislature passed an animal-abuse law that increased the fine for a second violation to $1,000 and two years in prison. At the same time the state's maximum penalty for second-offense spousal abuse is a mere $500 and six months.

King for a Day

We're all familiar with the fairy tale about a pauper waking up to find himself king. It really happened—and it happened in the United States. According to a nineteenth-century law no longer in existence, if neither the President nor the Vice President was in office, the president pro tem of the Senate became the commander-in-chief. On March 4, 1849, President James Knox Polk's term as President had expired, and the newly elected Zachary Taylor couldn't be sworn in because it was a Sunday. So for one remarkable and unusual day in American history, David Rice Atchison, who was the president pro tem of the Senate, officially became the President of the United States. What did Atchison do on his one day wielding supreme executive power? Nothing. He didn't know he had been the accidental President until several months later.

$400,000 added to an agriculture bill by Senate appropriator Daniel Inouye (D-Hawaii) for the Maui algal bloom crisis—even though there was no algal bloom crisis.

A Different Kind of Strip Mall

The Small Business Administration (SBA) is designed to help mom-and-pop businesses get on their feet by supplying loans, legal help, and information. In December 1994 the SBA's federal office in Birmingham, Alabama, announced that the newest entrepreneur to receive help was "Sammy's," a topless go-go bar located next to Westlawn Elementary School in Mobile. "[We] could not discriminate against them [just] because they are a go-go club," said the SBA director. The SBA can now get its honorary tassel.

It took over 299 years for our government to reach a national debt of $1 trillion (1982). It doubled in the next four years (1986), then doubled again to $4 trillion in 1992.

The Sting That Stung

California, 1994. It was a daring plan. It required catlike grace, the cunning of a mastermind, split-second timing, and flawless execution. Unfortunately, it was organized by a partnership between federal and state governments. The plan was to tempt alleged big-time drug traffickers with two hundred pounds of cocaine, courtesy of Uncle Sam. Once they took the bait, state and federal authorities would swoop down on the bad guys, make the streets safe, and make the news. The plan didn't include the bad guys getting away with the cocaine—but that's what happened: putting $4 million in premium grade cocaine out on the street. And they say it's the thought that counts.

"This strategy represents our policy for all time. Until it's changed."
—*Marlin Fitzwater, Bush White House spokesperson, on a just-released national security strategy (1990)*

Taking a Bad Thing Too Far

In 1988, a terrorist bomb exploded in the skies over Lockerbie, Scotland, killing everyone aboard Pan Am Flight 103. It was an unforgettable and unforgivable act of evil. But in November 1994 the U.S. government, specifically the Internal Revenue Service, took it one step farther. They mailed a letter to the brother of Mark Zwynenburg, one of the victims aboard flight 103, demanding money. The noticed stated, "In accordance with the provisions of the existing Internal Revenue laws, notice is hereby given that the determination of the estate tax liability discloses a deficiency of $6,484,339.39." That's not a typo. The IRS wanted their share of the money received from the lawsuit the Zwynenburgs filed against Pan Am airline and its insurer. (Pan Am went out of business shortly after the crash and re-formed on September 26, 1996.) Which is all well and good, except the Zwynenburgs haven't received one cent from the lawsuit. In fact, a settlement on the amount of money due the Zwynenburgs has never even been agreed upon. The Internal Revenue Service simply made a "guesstimate" that the final cash settlement (for the loss of Mark Zwynenburg's life) would be $11,702,925.00—and they wanted their cut within ninety days. Even after a public outcry the IRS refused to back down. John Zwynenburg, Mark's father, exclaimed, "I'll have to go out and hire my lawyer and my accountant to fight something that has no merit." A faceless government is one thing—but a heartless one?

The federal budget was last balanced in 1969.

Mud Pie, Anyone?

As noted throughout this book, the Environmental Protection Agency has been supervigilant in cleaning up the environment . . . even when it doesn't need to. Or, as former Interior Department chief economist Richard Stroup observed, "At one site EPA went to court and required parties to spend $9.3 million additional dollars to clean the site to a level where the dirt would be safe enough to eat for 260 days a year. (Safe enough to eat is the official standard on safe, uncontaminated soil.) EPA was unsatisfied with 'contaminated' dirt that everyone conceded was safe to eat for 70 days a year. And the site was in a swamp!" I would hate to see what they serve at an EPA luncheon.

Since 1984, taxpayers have paid $11 billion for the space station. The final projected cost is estimated at $94 billion—a 1,075 percent increase over the original price. To date, not a single piece of hardware has been built.

Crazy Hiring Practices

Disgruntled postal workers' turning violent has become so commonplace an event, even the worst stand-up comedians use it as comic material. But the Equal Employment Opportunity Commission created the ultimate "punch" line in hiring practices. A spring 1995 article in the *Employee Relations Law Journal* explains, "Many individuals who become violent toward customers or co-workers suffer from some form of mental disorder. Yet for an employer to be too careful in screening potentially dangerous persons out of the work force is to invite liability for discrimination under the ADA [Americans with Disabilities Act], while to be not careful enough is to invite tragedy and horrendous liability for negligent hire or negligent retention." Damned if you do, damned if you don't—and damned if it isn't just going to get worse.

"Obviously, I don't support it, but I support the impulses that are giving rise to it."
—Bill Clinton (Forty-second President), on the 1995 balanced budget amendment

It's the Great Pumpkin

Good consistency means that the canned pumpkin...after emptying from the container to a dry-flat surface...holds a high mound formation, and at the end of two minutes after emptying on such a surface the highest point of the mound is not less than 60 percent of the height of the container.

—Defense Department specifications for canned pumpkin procurement, paragraph 52.2747

Since 1980, of the 1,275 hazardous waste sites on the Environmental Protection Agency's list only 80 have been cleaned up. Cost? Over $15 billion.

The Devil Made Me Do It

The military doesn't want to openly admit gays in their ranks, but they don't seem to mind a witch or two. In the 1980s the Pentagon paid Kirchner Associates $30,000 to supply military chaplains with instructions on how best to deal with members of different and unconventional religious sects. Among those listed were Pagans, Wiccans, the Council of Witches, and the Church of Satan. Don't ask, don't tell—and don't put a curse on the general.

Nearly $12.6 million in earthquake relief checks from 1994 have been returned uncashed to the Federal Emergency Management Agency, mainly by people who didn't ask for the money.

Not Your Average John

A throne costing $23 million must belong to someone like King Tut, right? Nope. Try NASA. In 1993 the General Accounting Office reported NASA spent $23 million for a prototype toilet for the space shuttle. The toilet costs overflowed by 900 percent because its designer, United Technologies Hamilton Standard, became backed up redesigning the toilet after astronauts demanded a manual flush instead of an automatic feature. The $23 million price tag doesn't put a lid on the toilet's true cost—an additional $7 million was needed to make the model fully operational. In its first spin around the world aboard the Space Shuttle Endeavor, mission control had to caution the astronauts to keep the toilet lid down when it wasn't in use. A $30 million toilet? NASA should be flushed with embarrassment.

Since 1975, 5 million new government
jobs have been created.

Me and My Beeeeş Mouth

The studio bustled with activity. Lights were focused as cameras rolled into position. Representative Martin Hoke (R-Ohio) was preparing to comment on the President's 1994 State of the Union address. This was his big moment. A young female producer placed a microphone on the representative and then walked behind him to make sure the transmitter was on. With her back to him, Representative Hoke turned to a fellow House member, cupped his hands in front of his chest, and remarked, "She has the beeg breasts." Of course Representative Hoke didn't know the director was doing a camera check and the camera was on and running the entire time. Now who's the bigger boob?

Here's a little more tit-for-tat about Representative Hoke. He made clear the reason he came to Washington was not for his political career—but for his social life. "I could date [newly elected congresswomen] Maria Cantwell or Blanche Lambert—they're hot," Hoke said to *The New York Times*. With more members like Hoke we should call it the "Frat House of Representatives."

Only the state of Georgia requires a majority (50 percent plus one vote) to elect members of Congress.

Full Court Press

Stop the presses!!! In his 168-page 1993 treatise *Creating a Government That Works Better and Costs Less,* Vice President Albert Gore, Jr., was made an honorary member of the "Hall of Shame." His booklet, geared at cutting government spending, wound up costing the taxpayers nearly four times as much as it should have. According to the Government Printing Office (which all branches of government must use for printed material, even though private companies charge less), each copy of the VP's report should have cost only ninety cents—but in fact cost four dollars. The manuscript "was produced on the best and most expensive Grade 1 coated paper in multiple ink colors, at Quality Level 2 [the scale is 1 to 5] on a rush schedule over the Labor Day weekend." The normal cost of such a printing would have been $54,091—the bill to the taxpayer was $168,915. And remember, the name of the report was *Creating a Government That Works Better and Costs Less.*

In 1993, Iowans amended their constitution, by a vote of 540,000 to 400,000, in order not to permanently disallow from public office any person who has engaged in a duel.

Stay Tuned for This Important Announcement

It doesn't always pay to advertise. Take for example the well-planned drug raid that was to take place at a Washington, D.C., public housing complex. Six months of preparation and hundreds of thousands of dollars went into organizing and preparing more than two hundred federal agents and city police officers. The agent in charge of the operation was driving to the staging area the morning of the raid when he heard about the proposed top-secret plan over the radio. Apparently the city housing agency had issued a press release the night before, which announced there was going to be a drug sweep the following morning. The entire operation had to be canceled. A spokesperson for the housing agency promised the mistake "in no way diminishes our commitment to assist law-enforcement agencies." With friends like these, who needs enemies?

In 1996, almost 60 percent of personal income taxes will go just to pay the interest on the national debt.

You Can Wait in the Sitting Room or Sit in the Waiting Room

In the waiting area, the first thing that strikes one's eye is the magnificent sixty-foot-long, jade-green couch costing $22,701. It's a wonderfully hand-crafted eight-piece sectional, made by a very prestigious San Francisco furniture store, seating thirty people comfortably. Overhead, two computerized skylights, priced at $64,000, track the sun and engulf the rooms with the warm California sun. On the left are meditation atriums: spacious, inviting, comforting, priced at a mere $70,000. Is this the home of some glamorous movie star? Maybe a retreat for the rich and famous? No, it's the city jail. Because of a San Francisco city ordinance specifying that up to 2 percent of the total cost of new public buildings be delegated to art furnishings, the new $53.5 million 440-bed city jail spent $600,000 on the aforementioned penal necessities. Sheriff Michael Hennessey was quoted as saying, "If you're going to spend fifty million dollars, why not make it look nice?"

The jail *is* nice but unfortunately the project was so over budget, the city didn't have sufficient funds to hire enough people to fully staff the facility.

"That's the most unheard-of thing I ever
heard of."

—*Senator Joseph McCarthy (R-Wisconsin), about a witness's testimony
during the infamous communist "witch-hunt" trials of the 1950s*

You Made Your Bed, Now *Lie* in It

David Bath, former Colorado state representative, was convicted on charges arising out of a 1991 orgy. A videotape was made of the "political party" which involved a seventeen-year-old boy. Bath, who was instrumental in pushing through legislation severely penalizing the exploitation of minors, was convicted under his own law.

In September 1993 the Occupational Safety and Health Administration (OSHA) in Washington, D.C., reported that it had issued sixty citations and levied $90,000 in fines at the Federal Building in Kansas City, Missouri, for noncompliance with OSHA guidelines. The Federal Building houses the regional OSHA offices.

A Reasonable Facsimile

When it comes to the military, "Just the fax, ma'am" isn't good enough. In 1992 Senator Carl Levin (D-Michigan) checked into reports that the Air Force was buying 173 custom-made fax machines by Litton Industries. These fax machines were specially designed to survive a nuclear blast. But the real blast was the cost—$73 million. On closer scrutiny Senator Levin realized that these costs were inaccurate; the Air Force was actually spending $94.6 million—or $547,000 per machine. Magnavox put in a bid to the Air Force for fax machines that met the required specifications and cost only $15,000 per unit. But unfortunately, the Magnavox model transmitted pages to "newspaper" quality while the half-million-dollar Litton fax machine transmitted to "magazine" quality. And let's face it, the last thing one needs to deal with during a nuclear war is a substandard fax.

In the 1960s the Department of the Interior office revealed a plan to flood the Grand Canyon for use as a hydroelectric plant.

Get a Grip

Many resolutions pass through the Texas State House, and Representative Tom Moore, Jr., was concerned at how little attention legislators paid to the bills on which they voted. So, in 1971, as a joke, he introduced a bill honoring Albert DeSalvo for his pioneering work in population control. De Salvo, the notorious Boston Strangler, confessed to killing thirteen women in the Boston area. Moore's bill commended the Boston Strangler for serving *"his country, his state, and his community.... This compassionate gentleman's dedication and devotion to his work has enabled the weak and lonely throughout the nation to achieve and maintain a new degree of concern for their future.... He has been officially recognized by the state of Massachusetts for his noted activities and unconventional techniques involving population control and applied psychology."*

The resolution passed unanimously.

"If crime went down a hundred percent, it would still be fifty times higher than it should be."

—*Councilman John Bowman on the high crime in Washington, D.C.*

Manna from Heaven

During times of turmoil and civil unrest in foreign countries the United States always tries to help in some way or another. Food, clothes, weapons, whatever it takes to help out the underdog. So it was business as usual in 1994, when a United States plane dropped relief supplies to Rwandan refugees during an emergency mission. A simple throw of the lever would release much needed supplies—but the lever was thrown a little late. Seventeen tons of corned beef, flour, and other foods bombarded the refugees, who had to take cover from this "supplies strike." A UN helicopter and a school were nearly destroyed, and several Rwandans were injured, but nobody was killed. That's the good ending to this story. The bad ending happened on the border of Turkey and Iraq shortly after the Persian Gulf War ended. The U.S. dropped pallets of supplies to aid Kurdish refugees but missed their drop-off spot and crushed eight Kurds to death.

The Pentagon admitted spending nearly $11 million employing psychics to provide military information.

But Is It Art?

The proposal in front of the Aurora, Illinois, council in January 1995 was whether to allow city-approved graffiti murals. Alderman Marc Roberts, 41, decided to take a bold stroke against the measure and passed around a few photos to see if his fellow council members would consider it art. They didn't. What he showed them were four photographs of himself posing nude on a North Carolina beach in 1976. One photograph showed him climbing a lifeguard's tower and the other one showed him with his legs apart. Mayor David Piece quickly called for Roberts's resignation. Alderman Roberts later voted with his fellow council members to censure himself, admitting he had overstepped the boundaries of decency and good taste. "We've always said a picture's worth a thousand words," said Alderman Tess Wackerlin. "But in this case, I think we'd rather have had the thousand words." Of course we all know good art should be placed in a nice frame and hung well.

A farm bill earmarked $500,000 to make a memorial out of the boyhood home of Lawrence Welk; sponsored by Senator Quentin N. Burdick (D-North Dakota).

The World's Most Expensive Hole in the Ground

It's called the Superconducting Supercollider (SSC), and it was one of the most expensive science projects ever attempted by the United States government. It was supposed to be the atom smasher to beat all atom smashers. The collider would take up fifty-four miles of underground tunnels. Its job was to accelerate and collide subatomic particles, breaking them down into smaller and smaller particles. Few congressmen knew its exact scientific purpose or what the possible benefits would be—but, boy, did it sound good. The buzz around Washington was "big science," but it would also provide "big business." Texas, which has more politicians than a pig has atoms, wrangled the superconductor for itself and the project started. It was estimated this huge hole in the ground would cost $38,500 per inch—but when the long arm of bureaucracy got involved, the project tripled in its estimated costs; from an initial proposal of $3.9 billion to $11 billion.

As a result of the price increases, the "radioactive" energy about the project began to wear off and Congress decided to close down the project. In October 1993 the collider collided with the final vote to break it down into nothing. So now the government has a $2 billion hole in the ground—actually, two billion six hundred forty million; the extra $640 million was the price to close down the project.

But leave it to good old American know-how to save the day. According to farmer Natesh Vashisht, who has shown an interest in buying the huge hole, the five miles of constructed tunnels, with its steady temperature, high humidity, and complete and total darkness would be a perfect place to grow his crop—mushrooms.

Like mushrooms the American taxpayer is usually kept in the dark and fed manure. Six months after Congress decided to kill the Superconducting Supercollider, evidence of the top quark—a particle of the atom that only the Superconducting Supercollider was supposedly able to detect—was discovered at the twenty-five-year-old Fermilab in Illinois.

In 1988 the U.S. Department of Energy spent $1.4 million sending out sixteen thousand copies of the entire twenty-five-pound, 8,800-page environmental impact study on the Superconducting Supercollider. By law they were only required to send out a brief summary of the study.

Government Nunsense

It's not nice to fool Mother Nature, and it's especially not nice to fool Mother Teresa—but that's exactly what city officials in New York City did. In the winter of 1988 Mother Teresa, the Nobel Prize–winner and head of the Missionaries of Charity, wanted to do something nice for the homeless in the city. She and the sisters of the Missionaries of Charity planned on renovating two fire-ravaged buildings on 148th Street to use as a homeless shelter. The shelter would provide temporary care for sixty-four homeless men, including food and job referrals. The mayor of New York City, Ed Koch, agreed on the plan with Mother Teresa and in September 1989 the Missionaries of Charity began repairing the fire-damaged buildings using some $500,000 that the charity had raised itself (no city money was used for the project). But the city government had to get involved with the project somehow—enter the New York City building codes. According to the codes every new or newly renovated multiple-story building must have an elevator. The nuns contested the code on two counts: one, the Missionaries of Charity, in addition to their vows of poverty, refuse the use of modern conveniences; and two, they couldn't afford the extra $100,000 the elevators would cost. The city was firm. The nuns promised if any handicapped residents lived in their building they would carry them upstairs if need be. Now enter Anne Emerman, the head of the New York City Office for People with Disabilities. "In India they carry people in off the street," she said, "but that's not acceptable in our society." With resistance from the city and resistance from the People with Disabilities, Mother Teresa and the Missionaries of Charity crossed themselves, then crossed off the idea of helping the homeless in New York City.

The Arkansas legislature designed a law that would prevent voter intimidation. Unfortunately, the law is written in a way that, if enforced, would make voting illegal. It reads: "No person shall be permitted, under any pretext whatever, to come nearer than fifty feet of any door or window of any polling room, from the opening of the polls until the completion of the count and the certification of the counted returns."

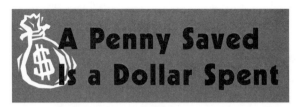

A Penny Saved Is a Dollar Spent

During the 1980s, efficiency experts saved the Department of Defense between $27 million and $136 million each year. However, the work of the efficiency experts cost between $150 and $300 million each year.

$19 million in federal funds to turn
Miami's plush Biscayne Boulevard into an
even more plush "exotic garden for
people to enjoy the richness of city life."

Computer Terminal Illness

The information superhighway recently took a turn for the worse thanks to the United States Treasury Department. With the best of intentions the Treasury Department wanted to educate computer security professionals about high-quality strains of computer viruses. They uploaded such viruses as "Satan's Little Helper," "Dark Avenger's Mutation Engine," and "The Internet Worm" onto the Department's Automated Information System computer bulletin board. To make sure the computer security professionals knew what they were up against, the Treasury Department also made available programs that are designed to make sneaking into other people's computers easier. For example, the "war dialer," software whose sole purpose is to find and store computer telephone numbers and "cracker software" used by computer hackers to break personal or secret access codes. What did these security professionals learn from this abundance of information? That the programs, since they were listed on the Automated Information System computer bulletin board, were available to anyone who decided to dial into the system. So for more than a year, over a thousand computer operators called up the bulletin board and were able to download strains of computer viruses that could completely disable computers and software and could turn anyone into "Super Hacker"—all courtesy of our government. Giving the term *computer nerd* a whole new meaning.

"The bottom line is there have been a lot of nuts elected to the United States Senate."

—Senator Charles Grassley (R-Iowa) in 1994, on why fellow Republicans shouldn't oppose Virginia GOP senate nominee Oliver North

Don't Leave Home Without It

In 1989 a private watchdog organization, the State Department Watch, issued a report about unusual or strange travel-expense reimbursements from the Department of State. According to the report, the Department of State issued eighteen thousand travel-expense checks without receipts or any evidence to justify the expenses. Would members of our government take advantage of something like this? One check for $9,000 was sent to "Ludwig van Beethoven," with a Social Security number of "123-45-6789."

$5 million approved by Congress to build a new Parliament building for the Solomon Islands. Even though it's part of the British Commonwealth.

When You Gotta Go—
You Gotta Go!

The Federal Occupational Safety and Health Administration, OSHA, stormed into Pro-Line Cap Company and demanded it do something about the women's rest room. In 1992 Pro-Line was cited for having too few toilets to accommodate its thirty female employees and OSHA wanted the situation rectified. The small Fort Worth, Texas, manufacturer couldn't afford the $25,000 renovation, much less to lose valuable production space—but they had to appease OSHA. And they did. They fired the thirty female employees. "We had two choices: to add toilets we could not afford or reduce the work force," Pro-Line attorney Franklin Sears said. "Adding toilets would take up needed production space, and we would have to lay off anyway even if we spent the money to comply with OSHA guidelines. Since the problem concerned only females, the only corrective action to take involved only females." Wonder what the EEOC had to say about that? They filed a complaint in January 1994. (The case was recently settled—the outcome was not disclosed.)

$100,000 to study the age-old problem of why people don't like beets.

Hidden Treasurer

Pull out any paper money that was printed while George Bush was in office (1988–1992) and you'll see the name Catalina Vasquez Villalpando. She served as treasurer of the United States and will now serve as the latest Treasure in the Big House for trying to "buck" the system. Villalpando was found guilty and sentenced to four months in prison for obstructing justice and conspiring to hide outside income. Maybe she was just collecting her own autograph.

"Capital punishment is our society's
recognition of the sanctity of human life."
—*Orrin Hatch (R-Utah), explaining his support of the death penalty*

Reach Out and Touch Someone

Just for fun, *Esquire* magazine ran a parody of a feed-the-hungry ad featuring superthin fashion model and Calvin Klein poster girl Kate Moss. The ad read, "*For just thirty-nine cents a day, less than the cost of a cup of coffee, you can keep this girl, and other supermodels just like her, alive. When you help sponsor a supermodel, you'll be providing essentials like warm miso soup and tuna carpaccio, a spare SoHo loft, and some truly spectacular clothing. Please help soon. Feed Kate Moss. Don't look away anymore.*" The ad included the toll-free number 1-800-SOS-WAIF. It just so happened that the number really belonged to the Federal Wage and Labor Law Institute in Houston, which received more than two thousand calls.

The El Paso, Texas, City Council approved $112,000 to retain a private security firm—to guard the city's police station.

Let's Make a Deal

Who came up with the idea for programs that encourage people to turn in their guns in exchange for money? The federal government, of course. For the last six years Congress has authorized more than $65 million to the Central Intelligence Agency so they can buy back more than a thousand Stinger missiles that they doled out to Afghan rebels during the 1980s confrontation with the Soviets. The fear is that these thirty-five-pound antiaircraft missiles will fall into the wrong hands or be sold to terrorists on the black market. A number of the missiles have appeared in Qatar, North Korea, and Iran and as many as four hundred unused Stingers remain in the hands of rebel forces. That's comforting to know. The United States Army originally paid $35,000 per missile from General Dynamics and simply handed them over to the Afghan rebels. In 1990, the CIA was offering $50,000 per missile in a buy-back program to beat all buy-back programs. But there weren't many takers at that price. Now, they're offering an estimated $100,000 per Stinger. Knowing the quality of lowest-bidder built Army weapons, just wait a few years and the new missile owners will be begging to give the things back.

In the 1985 Boise, Idaho, mayoral election, four write-in votes were received for Mr. Potato Head.

New and Improved

Finally, some truth in advertising. In 1990 the Strategic Air Command, headquartered in Omaha, Nebraska, decided to update its thirty-two-year-old motto, Peace is our profession. The new and improved motto, War is our profession—peace is our product was initiated by SAC commander General John T. Chain, Jr., who felt the new motto more closely represented the truth.

President Reagan gave a speech on the glories of freedom of the press during his 1983 visit to Japan. He demanded, however, that the entire speech be off the record.

How the Money Flies

In 1995 the National Science Foundation (NSF) handed over a $229,460 grant of taxpayer money so that scientists could study the sexual habits of houseflies. I'm sure it's been on the mind of most taxpayers what these little horny creature have been up to all these years. Experiments on some two thousand houseflies per week include: 1) creating transsexual male flies and 2) blinding other flies to discover how they mate using only their sense of smell. These studies might have some useful purpose: discover how they mate and find a way to use the knowledge against them as a form of pest control. But that's not what the study is about. In fact, there is no practical reason whatsoever for the study, except to examine the flies' "visual and chemical parts" of mating. What about if they smoke cigarettes and boast about their conquests to their little fly friends? Nope, none of these reasons. ". . . [W]e're looking at basic science here," said Gary Blomquist, the scientist heading the project. "I wouldn't even put a number on the years we need to study this. We're not even looking at control." Since when did the government decide that taxpayers should be in the business of pulling wings off flies? This was only the latest grant in a series that taxpayers have funded over the past fifteen years—for the same purpose.

In 1995, Dick Armey (R-Texas) meant to speak about openly gay congressman Barney Frank (D-Massachusetts)—but somehow the words *Barney Fag* accidentally slipped out.

Iron Bars Do Not a Prison Make

In 1995 officials of Duval County and Jacksonville, Florida, while beaming about their new $35 million jail, suddenly realized their "clink" was a "clunk." All 195 cells were relatively escape proof except for one small flaw—they didn't have any doors. City-county director of jails and prisons Michael Berg said he wasn't sure how the minor oversight occurred, but there was an additional $1.5 million left over to install the cell doors. Gee, I wonder where the extra money came from . . . perhaps the Prison-Cell-Door Fund?

Meanwhile, farther up the coast in Canandaigua, New York, they do have new prison-cell doors. Installation of these doors was halted, however, when officials of the Ontario County Jail realized the bars in the doors were so far apart, prisoners could simply slip through them. Makes you wonder if we're locking up the right people.

In the fall of 1992 Compton, California, mayor Walter R. Tucker III suggested that a local apartment building, where George and Barbara Bush lived for six months in 1949, qualify for national-landmark status. Unfortunately, at the time of the proposal, the apartment building was known by authorities as a local crack house.

Once Around
the Block, James

In 1995 Health Commissioner Barbara DeBuono, who advocated "streamlined" government and pushed for layoffs of department workers, hired a personal driver for herself through a temporary service and charged the $14.40 an hour to the department's tab. I wonder if she was a member of the Steering Committee?

Pete Domenici (R-New Mexico) pushed through the Senate a $100,000 grant to study the dangers of being hit by falling debris from disintegrating spacecraft. The study includes New Mexico residents only.

The Beat Goes On

The fact that the sixties are truly dead became apparent when Sonny Bono, of Sonny and Cher fame, was elected to Congress—as a Republican! In 1996, while explaining his allegiance to the Republican party, Representative Bono quipped that every time he deals with Democrats, "I feel like I have been kicked in the head." To which, Democratic Representative Melvin Watt quickly responded, "I just want the gentleman to know that there are a lot of people on this side who agree that you have been kicked in the head." He got you, babe.

According to the *Los Angeles Times,* while Sonny was mayor of Palm Springs, California (1988–1992), his public relations director, Marilyn Baker, had to rewrite his agendas into script form so Bono could conduct official business. "For call to order, I wrote, 'Sit.' For salute the flag, I wrote, 'Stand up, face flag, mouth words.' For roll call, I wrote, 'When you hear your name, say yes.'" She quit after three months. I guess she's no longer pro-Bono.

In the mid-1970s, the Law Enforcement Assistance Administration (LEAA) spent nearly $27,000 to determine why prisoners want to escape from jail.

The Government's Coming— Hide the Silverware!

In 1991 managers of the cafeteria located in the Treasury Department building issued a memo stating that: of the 2,040 individual pieces of silverware it owned, 1,430 pieces were missing and presumed stolen. Among other agencies, the building houses the IRS. But who's counting?

☆

"This is the worst disaster in California since I was elected."
—*California Governor Pat Brown, referring to a local flood*

Don't Do What I Say, Do What I Mean

Governor George Pataki of New York made an impassioned and uplifting speech at his 1994 inaugural address promising to put an end to "faceless government." He promptly locked the doors to the second floor of the Capitol, posted additional guards to protect him, canceled scheduled tours of the floor, and demanded the use of identification badges to gain admittance to the Capitol. Don't worry, his door is always open—you just have to get past the moat.

"It's a question of whether we're going to go forward into the future, or past to the back."

—*Vice President Dan Quayle (1988–1992)*

Going Up

When you're riding in an elevator looking at everything except the other people, it's reassuring to see the inspector's signature telling you the elevator is safe. The New Jersey Department of Consumer Affairs explained that, by law, all 567 towns in New Jersey must hire elevator inspectors. So why did the town councils of Upper Pittsgrove, Alloway, and Quinton, New Jersey, balk when they were told to hire elevator inspectors? Because their towns didn't have any elevators. Not one. When they explained this to the Department of Consumer Affairs, they didn't have to hire an inspector. Right? Wrong. "Otherwise," a spokesperson said, "the Uniform Construction Code would no longer be uniform." This kind of bureaucratic thinking pushes the "door close" button on logic.

"No sane person in the country likes the war in Vietnam, and neither does President Johnson."
—*Hubert Humphrey, Vice President under Lyndon B. Johnson*

A Burning Desire for Knowledge

We were all taught never to play with matches—but apparently the people at the Bureau of Land Management in Oregon didn't get that parental guidance. In a wildlife study at the Malheur National Wildlife Refuge near Frenchglen, Oregon, members of the study team started a "controlled" five-acre fire. The wind, however, did not cooperate with government regulations; the fire jumped the fire line, burned nine hundred acres of land, and destroyed a bird habitat. What was the theory they were so hot to investigate? Whether or not worms and other invertebrates emerged earlier in the year from scorched land. Now, thanks to a burning desire for more useless knowledge, the early bird won't be able to get the worm—because they've both been burned out of their homes.

$384,948 for the Department of Labor to count how many dogs and cats live in Ventura County, California.

The Fine of the Century

We all fear a notice from the IRS, especially when it reveals we owe back taxes. But the letter Dave Lampson received was a billion times worse—actually, 68 billion times worse. Lampson, a thirty-six-year-old systems engineer from Centerville, Virginia, is paying off an old $30,000 Internal Revenue Service debt in monthly installments of $500. But imagine his surprise when he received an updated bill for 68 billion dollars. That's not a typo. The bill was for 68 billion dollars. "It's mind boggling," Lampson said, according to an AP story. "That's more than my share of the national debt."

A spokesman for the IRS, Wilson Fadely, told *The Washington Post* that as many as one thousand erroneous bills with "very high figures" were sent from the agency's regional office in Kansas City, Missouri. The mistakes occurred because the IRS was actually doing something humane. They were reprogramming their central computer to stop sending bills to people in flood-ravaged states who had been paying their back taxes in installments. The biggest surprise to Lampson was the reaction he got when he called the Internal Revenue Service to correct the problem: "I talked to several people who didn't think it was out of line," Lampson said. "They were very nonchalant, as if I were questioning a hundred-dollar charge." Lampson figures he'll have his new tax bill paid off in approximately 11 million years—plus a few million more for late fees.

The United States Department of Agriculture spent $46,000 to calculate how long it takes to cook eggs.

You Can't Beat the Postal Service

Johnsonville, North Carolina. Four armed crooks raided a grocery store belonging to the town's postmaster and demanded he open the Postal Service safe and give them the contents. He refused. The gunmen pistol-whipped the postmaster, threatening to kill him and his wife, threatened to kill eight others in the store, and finally shot and wounded the man's son. The postmaster, realizing the few dollars' worth of stamps and money orders in the safe were not worth risking the lives of his family and customers, gave the crooks what they wanted. Not too soon after this harrowing experience, the U.S. Postal Service demanded the postmaster repay the forty-four dollars in stamps and money orders that were stolen from the grocery store safe. Why? Because as the Postal Service said, he failed to "exercise reasonable care." The postmaster paid. In my opinion he was a first-class male in a fourth-class service.

In 1992, record sales of $18.5 billion, more than double the previous year's total, officially made the United States the biggest supplier of weapons to the Third World.

Lost in Space

"One small step for man, one giant leap for mankind." These immortal words were transmitted through space in 1969—and there have been thousands of other transmissions since then. But according to a *Wall Street Journal* article, 90 percent of the data transmitted from NASA space missions has never been analyzed and cannot be analyzed. Why? Because the computer tapes on which the transmissions are stored (enough tapes to fill the fields of fifty football stadiums) can only be interpreted by computers that are now obsolete. Perhaps we should stop looking for intelligent life on Mars and start looking for intelligent life on our own planet.

"Anyone can be elected governor. I'm
proof of that."
—*Democrat Joe Frank Harris, two-term Georgia governor, about
who might replace him during the 1990 gubernatorial election*

Those Were the Days

In almost any business you can find people whose actions are a little underhanded. But politics seems to have a revolving door set up for these fellows. Elbridge Gerry had this to say about his fellow legislators from Massachusetts:

> ... Hence in Massachusetts the worst men get into the Legislature. Several members of that Body had lately been convicted of infamous crimes. Men of indigence, ignorance, and baseness, spare no pains, however dirty, to carry their point against men who are superior to the artifices practiced.

Sounds like something that was said last week, but Gerry spoke those words at the Constitutional Convention in 1787. The more things change—the more they stay the same.

During a trip to India, Jimmy Carter (thirty-ninth President), standing on the edge of a methane-generating pit of cow manure, heard ABC's Sam Donaldson say, "If I fell in, you'd pull me out, wouldn't you, Mr. President?" To which Carter replied, "Certainly . . . after a suitable interval."

Better Late than Never

In December 1992, in Berkeley, California, a postal carrier crashed into the car of Mr. Fran Ortiz, which was parked in front of Mr. Ortiz's house at the time. It wasn't a terrible accident; the postal worker wasn't hurt, and the United States Postal Service acknowledged complete responsibility, promising to pay $758 in damages. While filling out the damage claim, a Postal Service representative told Mr. Ortiz to expect "a long wait" before he received his reimbursement check. Ortiz understood the accounting process of most businesses, filed his claim, and left. In October 1993, ten months after submitting his claim, Ortiz still hadn't received his check so he called the Postal Service. He was told that the claim was still on the executive's desk and they would send it out immediately. Again he waited. When Mr. Ortiz did finally received the check on March 10 (fifteen months after the accident), he noticed the letter was postmarked February 24, 1994. What had caused the fifteen-day delay? Apparently his check had passed through the Dead Letter Office, been returned to the Postal Service, and then forwarded to Mr. Ortiz because the check had been inserted backward in the window envelope and no visible address could be seen. It has never been comforting to hear, "The check is in the mail," especially if it's the U.S. mail.

$2 million approved by Congress for a
skyway in Tacoma, Washington, created
so visitors could see Mount Ranier—
which is visible only about once a week.

The Boa Constricting Law

Philadelphia Councilman John F. Street sponsored a bill in 1987 that would prohibit people from carrying snakes on public streets and sidewalks, or in parks and other areas designed for recreation. According to *The Philadelphia Inquirer,* Street claimed the bill was needed because he was "tired" of seeing people carrying snakes in public. To most snake carriers this bill is a pain in their asp.

$11.5 million appropriated by the House
to modernize a power plant at the
Philadelphia naval yard—which is
scheduled to be closed.

Loyal as a Dog

It's hard to find dedicated employees these days. So people were amazed when Cook County (Chicago) board member and former Democratic Senator Ted Lechowicz volunteered to go to work at a six-week administrative job in the Illinois secretary of state's office after his term expired. What a guy. What a team player. What a crock. Owing to a loophole in the law, Lechowicz's temporary job qualified him to earn an extra $18,279 in pension income *every year for the rest of his life.* Some people might consider him clever—but his undeserved raise in pension is paid by the taxpayers of Illinois. When Lechowicz retired in 1995, after his six-week temp job, his pension was $61,200 per year—45 percent larger than the highest salary he ever earned as a state legislator. Of course, paying a government employee to do nothing is nothing new.

"My fellow Americans . . . I've signed legislation that will outlaw Russia forever. We begin bombing in five minutes."
—President Reagan, not realizing the microphone was on, shortly before a 1984 radio broadcast

If a Tree Falls in the Forest . . .

Congressman Neal Smith (D-Iowa) went out on a limb to be generous with the taxpayers' money. Smith set aside $15 million (the first installment of a $105 million four-year project) for states to hire small businesses to plant trees on state property. What a magnanimous decision. Except nobody wanted to do the project. The Small Business Administration, whose till Smith raided for the funds, didn't want to branch out into the tree-planting business, neither did the Small Business Committee in the House. But Smith kept barking out orders for the project, and since he chairs his own appropriations subcommittee, he simply wrote it into the budget before it went to a vote. When questioned by a reporter as to why Smith had funded the project when absolutely no one wanted it, the congressman replied, "Are you for tree planting or not?" Until this kind of bureaucratic robbery is put to an end Congress has got the taxpayer up a tree.

The National Institute of Neurological and Communicative Disorders and Stroke spent $160,000 to study if you can cast a spell on someone by drawing an X on his/her chest. Why? "The phenomenon under investigation," the Institute said, "cannot be understood or explained by information currently available and it is of obvious interest to determine what other heretofore unknown factors or mechanisms significantly influence muscle strength and movement."

The Light's Are on But Nobody's Home

Seems like Congress is in the dark when it comes to the real world, especially in the case of the Rural Electrification Administration (REA). The REA was established in 1935 as part of Franklin D. Roosevelt's New Deal. It was a wonderful plan that encouraged and helped rural Americans, mostly farmers, get electricity. The REA did this by lending money to small electric cooperatives at 2 percent interest, making electricity affordable to everyone. By 1950s, 90 percent of rural America had been electrified by the government plan. The 1960s saw the number of "lights on" houses reach 98 percent, and by the 1970s the number was 99 percent. So, the government achieved its goal, slapped itself on the back, and closed the Rural Electrification Administration down, right? Of course not. The government doesn't close useless, outdated departments—it expands them. The REA is still loaning out money, only now it's far below market rate, and the agency's losses are shocking. To date the REA has handed out guaranteed loans totaling $63 billion, with $36 billion still outstanding. With its original 1935 mentality this bureaucratic dynamo charges its borrowers only 5 percent interest—while the government pays 8 percent for its money. That's an improvement over the situation of the 1970s and 1980s; when the REA paid up to 12 percent for its money and loaned out cash for 5 percent. If Congress really wants to balance the budget, they need to turn off some lights and replace some of their own dim bulbs.

"I've spoken about a number of career opportunities, and one I've got to put into the blend is a prison ministry."
—*U.S. Representative and evangelist Patrick Swindall (R-Georgia), after being convicted on nine counts of perjury*

Nothing to Blow Your Nose At

Missouri State Representative Fred Williams introduced a bill in 1984 that would place a $200 fine on nose-blowing in restaurants if conducted in a "loud, obnoxious, or offensive manner." The "honker-halting" law was created by Williams after numerous unpleasant encounters with nose-blowers in restaurants, particularly at breakfast. Said Williams, "I've had to get out of a restaurant to keep from throwing up." Throwing up! There ought to be a law against that too!

☆

Lieutenant General Joseph Ashy spent $116,000 to fly himself and his cat from Italy to Colorado. The Pentagon said this was not a violation.

Location, Location, Location

"Location!" is the battle cry of anyone attempting to buy a new home. But thanks to the Department of Housing and Urban Development (HUD), reading about new homes or apartment rental listings in your newspaper may become a thing of the past. Taking political correctness to the extreme, HUD began cracking down on newspapers for their choice of words in describing apartments and homes. The Fair Housing Act Amendments of 1988 made it "*unlawful to make, print, or publish, or cause to be made, printed, or published, any notice, statement, or advertisement, with respect to the sale or rental of a dwelling, that indicates any preference, limitation, or discrimination because of race, color, religion, sex, handicap, familial status, or national origin.*" Phrases such as *master bedroom* are considered racist; *walk-in closet* discriminates against people in wheelchairs, even references to houses of worship are considered taboo. "*References to a synagogue, congregation, or parish may . . . indicate a[n illegal] religious preference. Names of facilities which cater to a particular racial, national origin, or religious group such as country-club or private-school designations . . . may indicate a[n illegal] preference.*" Pretty soon, if HUD continues to get its way, an advertisement for a house will read, "House."

**Congress spends an average of $1.58
for every dollar raised in new taxes.**

The Final Debate

In 1978 Joe Taylor, a Republican candidate for county sheriff in Washington state, was campaigning at a candidates' forum and vehemently criticizing his opponent, Detective John Kozar. Suddenly, Taylor suffered a massive heart attack and fell to the floor. Kozar and Sheriff Bill Williams administered heart massage and mouth-to-mouth resuscitation in a failed attempt to revive Taylor. "Death is death," said Williams. "It transcends politics."

There are more than 500,000 elected officials in the United States.

Throwing in the Towel

To commemorate the fiftieth anniversary of D-Day, President and Mrs. Clinton, along with forty advisors and twenty-three journalists, crossed the English Channel aboard the U.S. aircraft carrier *George Washington.* It was a emotional event and there wasn't a dry eye in the house. Maybe that's what accounted for allegations from an internal U.S. Navy memo that claimed sixty-eight towels and sixteen bathrobes had gone overboard with the President and his crew. The Navy billed President Clinton's office $562 for the terry-cloth take-home. In order to find these robe robbers, two of the President's trip planners wrote memos to staff members who had crossed the English Channel, to cough up the stolen linens. "A number of items were removed from staterooms on the ship during the White House visit," they wrote. "The following items are unaccounted for: thirteen blue towels with *GW [George Washington]* insignia—$1 each; four *GW* bathrobes with insignia—$35 each; twelve plain white bathrobes—$15 each; fifty-five white towels—$.80 each." Maybe when the President's staff heard there were complimentary bathrobes—they took it literally.

"I'm gonna be so tough as mayor I'm gonna make Attila the Hun look like a faggot."

—*Philadelphia Police Commissioner Frank Rizzo during his successful 1971 campaign for mayor*

There's No Place Like Home

La Jolla, California, is a very exclusive, very rich suburb of San Diego. Living there means you've made it. Recently there has been constructed an additional twenty-eight-unit apartment complex, with market values between $300,000 to $500,000 each. These luxury apartments are exquisitely furnished and boast panoramic 180-degree views of the Pacific Ocean. So imagine the surprise when the Department of Housing and Urban Development handed the keys to these apartments to a group of twenty-eight welfare-recipient families—some with incomes as high as $34,000. That's right. HUD thought it wouldn't be fair to welfare recipients if places like La Jolla were out of their price range, forgetting that $500,000 apartments are out of the range of the majority of hard-working ordinary folks too. But HUD, obviously from another world, thought this is how our tax money should be spent. The public housing tenants will typically pay around $323 a month; although some will pay up to $675 a month, depending on their income. I believe all Americans are for helping the less fortunate, but to make the less fortunate the most fortunate doesn't seem fair either. It is, after all, called "fair housing," isn't it?

$105,163 was spent, courtesy of a federal grant, to study the "Evolution of Monogamy in Biparental Rodents."

Eat, Drink, and Be Wary

The Food and Drug Administration (the people who approved Red Dye #40, then took it away, then brought it back, and are now talking about taking it away again) are still hard at work. It's comforting to know there's an agency making sure our food is uncontaminated, our prescription drugs are safe, and our medical devices are manufactured properly. However, what the FDA considers medical devices to be and what the normal, everyday, run-of-the-mill American citizen might consider medical devices to be are worlds apart. Products that require FDA approval before being sold include: wheelchair cushions, McDonald's sunglasses, low-pressure mattresses, dental bibs, New Freedom ultra-thin pads, Super Poli-Grip denture adhesive cream, spectacle frames, dental trays, mint-flavored dental floss, and an Amish country spa. While they've been busy approving these items for our safety, the FDA has dragged its heels approving a cardiopump that is already widely used in Europe. An estimated twenty-eight thousand heart attack victims who could have been saved by the cardiopump have died during the last four years. Why is the FDA holding back its approval? The administration continues to insist that pump makers get the "informed consent" of any person on whom the pump may be tested. But many heart attack victims (people who are clinically dead because their heart has stopped beating) have a hard time giving their consent. I can't believe the nerve of these heart attack victims holding back progress like that.

Missouri state legislators approved a five-pound 1,012-page bill aimed at reducing state paperwork.

A Taxing Situation

Normally when we think of the IRS making a mistake, we think it's going to be against us. Well, that wasn't the case with Joseph H. Hale. While Mr. Hale was cooling his heels in federal prison on fraud charges, the IRS was trying to collect $2 million in back taxes from him. Instead they wound up sending him a check for $359,380.25. Once they realized they had made a "computer error" the IRS wanted their money back, but Mr. Hale had other ideas. A federal grand jury charged that a friend of Hales had helped him hide the money and indicted them both. After two years of painstaking detective work, the IRS found only $55,558.34 of the money. During the court proceedings it was uncovered that while in prison Hale filed a tax refund claim, the IRS honored it, and that's why the original check was received. And they say you can't teach a jailbird new tricks.

"We must restore to Chicago all the
good things it never had."

—*Richard Daley, mayor of Chicago*

Hitler Was Just a Misunderstood Man with a Mustache

A panel organized by the U.S. Department of Education debated the then upcoming 1986 student history curriculums. One curriculum was designed to illustrate the Holocaust in Nazi Germany in which 6 million Jews died during World War II. The panel issued their report criticizing the content of the curriculum. They said it was "unfair" to Nazis because "the program gives no evidence of balance or objectivity." Remember, the U.S. Department of Education sets forth the standards that all school curriculums must meet.

$10,400,000 fought for by House appropriator Norm Dicks (D-Washington), and finally approved by the House, for a physical-fitness center at Bremerton Puget Sound Naval Shipyard—even though there are five gyms within a five-minute drive of the shipyard.

You Want Fries with That?

The United States has always been a big brother to other countries. When people are in distress, we're there. So before the government sent troops to Somalia, they needed to find a way to stop the theft of food shipments being sent to the Somali people. The plan was ingenious. The government decided to send the Somalis food they don't like—that way the rebels wouldn't steal it and sell it on the black market. According to Andrew Natsios, assistant administrator of the Agency on International Development, corn and sorghum were sent because they served two purposes: one, they are nutritious enough to ward off starvation; and, two, they aren't popular enough to command decent black-market prices.

Number of Susan B. Anthony dollars held
by the federal government: 248,100,000.
Cost per year to store them: $30,000.

Eight Days a Week

How hard do state senators work? Ohio's state senate claims it was in session 362 days in 1993—including Saturdays, Sundays, Christmas, Memorial Day and Thanksgiving. In fact these senators, most of whom have other jobs, tell the IRS with a straight face that the only days they weren't in session were January 1 and January 2. There's a little kink in the law that helps these hardworking senators: it's called a "skeleton session." Here's how it works. Usually on Thursdays, only two senators will show up. One senator calls the session to order. A clerk reads a few things into the record, making it seem like they're doing something, and then the only other member present moves to adjourn. Once the Senate is in session, it is considered in session for five days in a row—even if no one is there. And with enough skeleton sessions it's easy to see how they can meet for 362 days out of the year. The bonus to this practice is that there's a federal law on the books that allows state legislators to reduce their federal income taxes for every day they are in session, if they live more than fifty miles from the state's capital building. Senator Bob Nettle, who also runs a tax business with his wife, says the exaggerated deduction is "absolutely ridiculous" and so unethical, he won't claim it. He tallied up the actual time in session to be about two hundred days a year—and that's the number he's claiming on his tax form. There's something you don't hear about that often—an honest senator.

One of the EPA's largest contractors invoiced $2.3 million for tickets to sporting events, company parties, and travel by employee spouses. How did the EPA deal with this? They paid.

Sounds Like a Fair Trade

Children have made trades for years: "I'll trade you my peanut butter sandwich for your frog." But the federal government likes to complicate matters—no matter how uncomplicated they should be. Here's an example of how the United States makes trades with other countries.

> *Notwithstanding any other provision of law, no trade benefit shall be extended to any country by reason of the extension of any trade benefit to another country under a trade agreement entered into under paragraph (1) with other such country.*
> —Excerpt from the Trade Bill in the Senate, Section 4602

Israelis on the West Bank of Israel got $3.5 million for two Orthodox religious schools and a teacher training facility courtesy of the United States government (in other words, the taxpayers).

The Currency Exchange

According to the "Report to Congress on the Activities and Operations of the Public Integrity Section (1993)," a yearly report that chronicles illegal activities for people on the public payroll, Jean Marie Boswell pleaded guilty to having stolen $14,520 in government funds. She admitted that during 1992, while working as a secretary and cash custodian to a Department of Defense facility in Atlanta, she opened two packages containing $100 and $50 bills. She replaced $1 bills for all but the bigger bills on the top and bottom, put the money back, and resealed the package. It wasn't until Boswell left government service that her little sleight-of-hand trick was discovered. As part of her plea agreement on October 12, 1993, Boswell agreed to repay the $14,520. One word of advice: Be sure to count the money first.

In Vermont the EPA spent $38,174 to discover that runoff from stacks of cow manure polluted nearby streams and ponds.

A Sign of the Times

Over ten years ago the federal government adopted universal symbols to replace words on street and traffic signs—another contribution to the dumbing of America. But traffic signs depicting a stooped figure, warning motorists of elderly pedestrians, were rejected by officials from Pennsauken, New Jersey—because they feared it would be a clear sign to criminals that there were elderly people in the neighborhood.

**"The present system may be
flawed, but that's not to say that we
in Congress can't make it worse."**
*—Representative E. Clay Shaw (R-Florida) in 1994,
during the debate on health-care reform*

Buttering Up Congress

In February 1996 the Senate passed a groundbreaking farm bill that would eliminate a lot of nonsensical federal subsidies for farmers (i.e., mohair production, squash subsidies, et cetera). But planted deep in the furrows of the farm bill was a little attachment that will soon create yet another committee, the Federal Popcorn Board. This board's job will be to promote this lighter-than-air snack that has been doing extremely well, especially after the FDA scared theaters into using canola oil. Senate Agriculture Committee Chairman Richard G. Lugar (R-Indiana) had the kernel of an idea for the Popcorn Board along with the Popcorn Institute, a trade association. The following are excerpts from Sections 901 and 902 (a) of the Popcorn Act.

> Subtitle A—Popcorn
> SEC. 901. SHORT TITLE
> This subtitle may be cited as the "Popcorn Promotion, Research, and Consumer Information Act."
> SEC. 902. FINDINGS AND DECLARATIONS OF POLICY.
> (a) FINDINGS—Congress finds that—
> (1) popcorn is an important food that is a valuable part of the human diet;
> (2) a production and processing of popcorn plays a significant role in the economy of the United States in that popcorn is processed by several popcorn processors, distributed

through wholesale and retail outlets, and consumed by millions of people throughout the United States and foreign countries;

(4) the maintenance and expansion of existing markets and uses and the developments of new markets and uses for popcorn are vital to the welfare of processors and persons concerned with marketing, using, and producing popcorn for the market, as well as to the agricultural economy of the United States.

What's next—the Federal Milk Dud, Cracker Jack, and Goobers Board?

In 1957 Strom Thurmond (R-South Carolina) set the U.S. record for a "filibuster." A "filibuster" is when a member of Congress holds the floor by speaking nonstop; usually so that voting on a particular bill will be delayed until the following session. His record: twenty-four hours and eighteen minutes.

All's Well That Ends Welfare

Winning the lottery, inheriting money, or receiving an insurance settlement may seem like the road to financial independence—especially if you're on welfare. So what advice did the Western Massachusetts Legal Services Corporation give welfare recipients who hit the jackpot? Spend the money as fast as you can so you can stay on the welfare rolls. Under the bylaws of the welfare department, people on public assistance are allowed to collect cash windfalls without losing their benefits for more than a month. If you know you're about to receive additional income, the Legal Service brochure describes how to get off welfare the month before so you can spend the money without restrictions. "Prepay a portion of your rent or mortgage so that you can use the [welfare money] for other things." The brochure also suggests that you "buy a special gift, take a vacation, [or] put [the newfound money] into savings." Using the money to live on, investing for your future, and getting off public assistance aren't mentioned in the brochure, which, by the way, was paid for with taxpayer money.

The U.S. military operates 234 golf courses.

Political Ammunition

During the 1992 race for the Florida state legislature, Democrat Eric Adam Kaplan decided to give his lackluster campaign a shot in the arm—well, actually it was a shot in the leg. Seminole County Democratic party officials had criticized Kaplan for dragging his heels during the campaign and not sparking any interest in the party. "He hasn't done anything," complained one volunteer. "He's done no advertising." Seminole County is a heavily Republican district and Kaplan figured it was time to do something drastic: and he did. Kaplan was arrested and charged with firing five shots into the home of his opponent, Robert Starks. Mr. Starks's wife, Judith Starks, was hit in the leg by one of the bullets while she slept. Kaplan withdrew from the race. "We believe he wanted to win in the worst way," said Sheriff Don Eslinger. When it comes to running for state legislature, you can't say Eric Kaplan didn't take a shot at it.

Ratio of lobbyists to senators in Washington, D.C.: seventy-four to one.

Smearing It on Thick

People seem to be tired of negative political advertisements. But the ad produced by George Smathers, who ran against incumbent Democratic Senator Claude D. Pepper, deserves a rerun.

> *Are you aware that Claude Pepper is known all over Washington as a shameless extrovert? Not only that, but this man is reliably reported to practice nepotism with his sister-in-law, and he has a sister who was once a thespian in wicked New York. Worst of all, it is an established fact that Mr. Pepper, before his marriage, habitually practiced celibacy.*

This is a classic example of political double-talk from a campaign that occurred over forty-five years ago.

"If there is death, if death occurs, the death penalty is available, and we will seek it."
—*Janet Reno on whether she would seek the death penalty for the Oklahoma bombers: May 1995*

It's Just Like Boys' Town

"Out of fifty-nine thousand students who have graduated from a variety of programs, less than three hundred have been cited for human rights violations like torture and murder, and less than fifty have been convicted of anything."

—Major Gordon Martel, spokesman for the U.S. Army's School for the Americas, answering allegations that the school is actually a training center for assassins

$5 million by the Senate for the High Frequency Active Auroral Research Project in Alaska—basically, trapping energy from the Aurora Borealis. The additional funds were requested by Senate appropriator Ted Stevens (R-Alaska).

Smokey, Baby, Sweety!

A U.S. Forest Service employee oversees the government trademark on Smokey the Bear, acting, in effect, as the character's manager. As of 1989 the position paid $42,000 per year. "Only You Can Prevent Government Waste!"

"I'm not indecisive. Am I indecisive?"
—*Jim Seibel, mayor of St. Paul, Minnesota*

A Huge Slice of the Pie

If you're ever in Rhode Island munching on a medium pizza-with-everything, be careful—you may be contributing to a federal offense. In March 1994 *The Providence Journal-Bulletin* reported that the Internal Revenue Service office in Rhode Island was zeroing in on tax underpayments by pizza parlors. These mathematical madmen have come up with an ingenious way to figure out how much dough the pizza parlors make so they can have their slice of the pie. The IRS calculated a standard amount of flour in a pizza, divided that number by the total amount of flour purchased by the restaurant, compared that to the actual number of pizzas made, and then determined the projected income of the store. If their figure was more than the figure the pizza parlor was reporting, the store had to deliver the extra taxes to the IRS: probably within thirty minutes or less.

In 1993, the Environmental Protection Agency (EPA), responded to a congressional report claiming the agency uses too many outside contractors. The EPA paid $20,000 for a contractor to write the report.

A Flood of Money and Drugs

When it rains, it pours—money, that is. Several counties in Wisconsin were flooded in 1993 but Milwaukee County, Wisconsin, wasn't one of them. Even so, they were offered a $50,000 federal grant for flood damage. The county's Department of Human Services asked if the money could go to other areas of the state that had actually suffered some flood damage, but the federal government said no. And, in its infinite wisdom, the feds earmarked the money for a specific purpose. Was it to help stimulate the economy, help feed fictitious flood-victims, or buy clothes? Nope. The money could only be used for treating flood-related drug and alcohol abuse by residents in parts of Milwaukee County. "Is it federal philosophy that if your basement was flooded, it may lead you to drinking and you could get federal money?" asked county supervisor Lynne DeBruin during a meeting of the county board's health committee. "It probably was," said an embarrassed Patricia J. Towers, director of adult services for the Department of Human Resources. Problems like these rear their ugly head because Washington is too far away from the people it represents. Thankfully cooler and more sober heads at the local level can rail against bureaucratic boondoggles. Both DeBruin and county executive F. Thomas Ament vetoed acceptance of the funds. I'll drink to that!

$220,000 approved by the Senate for lowbush blueberry research. Since 1990, $950,000 has been appropriated for such research.

A Lot of Words—a Little Meaning

On December 4, 1980, the presiding officer in the Senate announced, "A quorum is present." A "vote" was called and the presiding officer announced the motion up for vote, which was: "The question is on agreeing to the motion to lay on the table the motion to reconsider the vote by which the motion to lay on the table the motion to proceed to the consideration of the fair housing bill was rejected. On this question, the yeas and nays have been ordered, and the clerk will call the roll." The legislative clerk did his duty, called the roll, tallied the votes and announced the results: Yeas, 61; Nays, 31. So, according to the *Congressional Record,* "the motion to lay on the table the motion to reconsider the vote by which the motion to lay on the table the motion to proceed to the consideration of the fair housing bill (H.R. 5200) was rejected was agreed to." With this much mouth motion to consider, I'll have to lay on the table.

"I feel a little like Zsa Zsa Gabor's fifth husband. I know what I'm supposed to do, but I'm not sure I know how to make it interesting."

—*Senator Albert Gore (D-Tennessee) in 1988, at a Democratic party function, on following twenty-three previous speakers*

It's Not Nice to Fool Mother Nature

What picturesque section of the United States looks like it was painted with an artist's brush? I'll give you a hint, it's not Arizona's famous painted desert. It's rock faces along national highways. In 1995 Representative Jack Metcalf (R-Washington) uncovered a government-sponsored program he doesn't have a palate (or is it palette?) for—painting rock faces exposed by construction or landslides to make them look older. "I said it can't be true. Nobody is that stupid," said Metcalf. He persuaded the U.S. Forest Service and the Washington State Department of Transportation to temporarily halt plans to paint rocks on a highway that ran through his home state. To his amazement Metcalf found out that "rock colorization" projects have become fairly routine along national scenic highways. The one he postponed would have dyed rocks in grays and browns along a section of U.S. Highway 2 where it crosses the Cascade Mountains. The initial bid for this project was $18,000, but that price escalated to $37,000 by the time the final bid was accepted. "This is a prime example of government run amok," Metcalf said. Rock colorization, just another brush with the sketchy mentality of some bureaucrats.

$10 million was secured by Senator Robert Kasten (R-Wisconsin) to build a ramp to the Milwaukee Brewers stadium parking lot.

One Potato, Two Potato

The military runs on its stomach, so when an urgent call came from the Air Force, a trucking firm in Grand Forks, North Dakota, jumped into action. A truck and driver were needed to take an emergency load of potatoes to a military depot in Dallas, Texas. Frantic to get this done ASAP, the trucking firm tried to find an available driver. Everyone was on assignments, but one good civilian took leave from retirement to make the run. He picked up the load at the shipping dock in Grand Forks and drove to Dallas to deliver the spuds on time. While he watched the crew unload the potatoes, pleased with himself that in his own special way he had helped our military, the Grand Forks driver asked one of the workers, "Where are these potatoes headed?" The response was quick and mind boggling: "Grand Forks Air Force Base." Military intelligence? You be the judge.

Texas Senator David Sibley, describing tough negotiations in February 1995 on pending state tort reform legislation: "It was like playing Pick-Up-Stix with your butt cheeks."

Makes Sense to Me

Communications is the most important element of any business—especially in this age of worldwide communication and the information superhighway. This memo from the Office of Management and Budget (OMB) gives us a clear picture of how things are done in Washington.

An agency subject to the provisions of the Federal Reports Act may enter into an arrangement with an organization not subject to the Act whereby the organization not subject to the Act collects information on behalf of the agency subject to the Act. The reverse also occurs.

Sometimes I think aliens have landed and set up shop in our nation's capital.

☆

In May 1995 the Republican party of **Virginia set up a six-thousand-seat convention hall and held an open house in Richmond to attract black voters. Nine people showed up.**

An Alien Concept

Freedom of speech and peaceful assembly are guaranteed under the First Amendment to the Constitution of the United States. It was put first because our forefathers were tired of being gagged by the king of England and didn't want that right to be taken away from the people of the new colonies. But Washington Congressman Albert Johnson, chairman of the House Committee on Immigration, has a different spin on the First.

"Let me tell you that tolerance is one thing, intolerance another. To be a person intolerant of another person's right to have different views is my idea of tolerance, that is, until that person endeavors to make a public issue of his views." A public issue—such as making a speech like this?

Automotive dismantler and recycler.
            —Pennsylvania legislature term for Junkyard

The Words Just Dribble off His Tongue

"I think today that a few remarks I might make, we go back to the relationship in this great nation with the people who was the foundation of America, the people they've paid such a price that we may enjoy the blessings of enjoyment that we have, has been spoken this morning."
—Evan Mecham, former Republican governor of Arizona

Mecham won a three-way race in 1986 and became governor with only 40 percent of the vote. He immediately raised eyebrows and a ruckus when one of his first acts as governor was to repeal the state's Martin Luther King Holiday. This prompted a boycott of the state by various conventioneers and showed that some people would rather hate than get a paid holiday off work. *Mecham* rhymes with *impeach 'em*—which is just what happened to the governor in April 1988.

In his or her lifetime the average American works 24,000 hours earning the money to pay taxes.

Squash, Anyone?

"America needs more squash!" must have been the battle cry of Mitchell County, Georgia. In 1992 Mitchell County, the nation's squash capital, planted over ten thousand acres of the yellow gourd, twenty times the acreage planted in the 1980s—and more than any other county in America. But the crop didn't grow quite as they expected. It didn't help matters that some farmers planted too early; others too late; some didn't irrigate the soil or used cheap seeds. Eventually, however, their cash crop did come in, a whole bushel of federal disaster aid. According to the General Accounting Office, the Agriculture Department farmed out $814.8 million for disaster aid on 847 specialty crops between 1988 and 1993. 1993 saw $96,467 go for rutabaga, $14,443 for an exotic fruit called pummelo, and $614,377 for an American staple, ginseng root. The list has ranged from extra-large tropical fish to catnip. Of course, not all farmers are tilling the fertile valleys of our nation's pocketbook—but a few are. A Senate study put the amount of illegally harvested federal funds for nine states between 1988 and 1993 at $92.5 million. Even though local farmer committees are supposed to catch such "crop tendering," nearly a hundred farmers in Mitchell County requested disaster aid for their sick squash. "Everybody got on the bandwagon," says committee member Crawford Smith. "I think ninety percent of the disaster claims were true. But I didn't just fall off a turnip truck. . . . Some abused the hell out of it." So for some devious farmers, even when their crops turn brown, they still harvest the green.

There are approximately 85,000 different levels of governments in the United States government; including federal, state, city, county, et cetera.

Five of One, Half Dozen of Another

In 1991 Democrat Edwin W. Edwards, while running for governor of Louisiana against former KKK honcho David Duke (Republican), invited his constituency to write his campaign headquarters for his "comprehensive ten-point plan to improve education." Those who did were delivered a plan containing exactly nine points. When politicians involve themselves in education—nothing adds up. Edwards won the election even though he spent much of 1986 and 1987 under trial for bribery charges (on which he was acquitted). With the choice of candidates being between Duke, the founder of the National Association for the Advancement of White People, and Edwards, who was plagued with ethics violations, supporters of Edwards proudly displayed bumper stickers that read VOTE FOR THE CROOK. IT'S IMPORTANT.

In the 1996 federal budget $3,758,000 was added by the Senate for "Wood utilization research." Since 1985, $35,015,000 has been funneled into the research.

Mom, Apple Pie, and Borscht

According to a former FBI agent, during the early 1990s the Federal Bureau of Investigation had 1,500 informants in the American Communist party. Since all their informants paid dues, the U.S. government was the largest financial supporter of the American Communist party, second only to the Soviet Union. That fact made everyone at the FBI a little Red in the face.

☆

"The thought of being President frightens me and I do not think I want the job."
—*Ronald Reagan in 1973*

Waltzing into Trouble

On July 28, 1993, a jury found former senior intelligence analyst for the Defense Intelligence Agency Peter L. Collins guilty of converting government property. He admitted to using a highly classified secure DIA computer system and government photocopiers for activities unrelated to official government business. Was this man a spy? A covert operator smuggling high-security government plans out of the DIA? Nope. Collins used the DIA computer system over a period of several years to create newsletters and lengthy calendars to promote his amateur ballroom dance association. Collins two-stepped his way into using DIA photocopiers and published the number of a DIA fax machine as the fax number of his dance association. On November 4, 1993, Collins tangoed into court and was sentenced to one year of unsupervised probation.

The IRS penalized George Wittmeier $159.78 for not paying all his taxes. Wittmeier underpaid by a penny.

Let Me Make One Thing Perfectly Clear

Not only do you have to be a mathematical wizard to figure out the IRS tax codes—you also have to be an ace detective. Here's an example from the code that would make even Sherlock Holmes's head explode. From Section 509 (a), which deals with the definition of a private foundation, I quote: "For purposes of paragraph (3), an organization described in paragraph (2) shall be deemed to include an organization described in section 501 (c) (4), (5), or (6) which would be described in paragraph (2) if it were an organization described in section 501 (c) (3)." So, in accordance with this article (D) of the IRS code (U) formulas (M) described in (B), are equated as (D)(U)(M)(B).

The Air Force spent $100,000 to blast simulated jet engine noise through barns to see how it affected pregnant horses. Result? They didn't like it.

The Pre-Post Office

Complaints about slow postal workers are common. So you would think the post office would attempt to overcome this negative impression. In August 1994 postal clerk Joannie McCaughey and three others at the post office in Cambridge, Massachusetts, were handed formal reprimands by their supervisor. It was a time-clock violation. "Future deficiencies . . . will result in more severe disciplinary action," read the memo, "including suspension or removal from the Postal Service." Finally, management is cracking down on postal workers arriving late for work. Not quite. The reprimand was for punching in at 8:59 when the shift didn't begin until 9:00. Cambridge postal supervisor Michael Hannon said, "It would become an abusive situation," if every employee were unprofessional enough to punch in one minute early every day. Now the whole disgruntled-postal-worker thing begins to make sense.

☆

In 1989, Washington State Senator Jim West proposed legislation to make it illegal for couples under eighteen to engage in "heavy petting." The bill was killed the next year.

A Shocking Statement

In 1995 Gulf States Energy sent Jimmy and Tammy Cobb, owners of Vidor Hardware Store, an August electric bill totaling $11,227,379.30. After the Cobbs protested, their next bill showed they didn't owe the $11 million; they now had a credit of $27,488.79. If I didn't know any better I'd think the Rural Electrification Administration was involved.

$8 million worth of foreign aid was requested by Congress to build religious schools for North African Jews living in France. The bill was withdrawn.

Uranium Ore Bust

Never before in the history of the United States has the threat of terrorism been so imminent. Airport security has tightened twentyfold; assault weapons have been banned; there are metal detectors at major governmental buildings; and guards posted everywhere. Everyone seems to be doing their part. Except maybe the Department of Energy (DOE). In 1993 Idaho scrap-metal dealer Tom Johansen purchased state-of-the-art nuclear reprocessing equipment from a DOE surplus sale. Johansen also obtained operating instructions for creating bomb-grade uranium with his newly purchased equipment simply by paying DOE a $280 photocopying fee. The sale went through without a hitch because the DOE man responsible could not persuade his "superiors" (and I use the term begrudgingly) how utterly stupid and completely inappropriate it was to sell such dangerous materials. It seems like the DOE was more interested in getting some M-O-N-E-Y than providing national security.

Congress appropriated $80,000 to determine if floss from milkweed pods could replace goose down in bedding.

One Vote Can Make the Difference

We've all heard the expression Every vote counts. And for Denny James, who was running for board of aldermen of Centerville, Mississippi, the expression couldn't have been more true. According to a January 1992 article in *Parade* magazine, Mr. James looked like a "sure thing" for the aldermanship because he was the only candidate. Everyone went about their daily lives confident their neighbor would vote for James; even James himself didn't make it to the polls that day. Later in the evening, when the results were in, the town was shocked to see the final count—0. No one voted. State law says a candidate must receive at least one vote before declaring victory, so another election was held. James put on a serious get-out-the-vote campaign. It was successful; he won with a whopping forty-five votes.

$60,000 in federal grant money to the University of Massachusetts to study Belgian endive.

Letting It All Hang Out

There couldn't be a nicer-sounding town in America than Friendsville. The fine people of Friendsville, Maryland, will give you the shirts off their backs and their mayor has nothing to hide. In fact, he's a little more open to the public than most people would like. In February 1995 Mayor Spencer Scholsnagle pleaded guilty to one count of exposing himself in his car on Interstate 68. This followed an earlier conviction on the same charge—on the same stretch of road. Scholsnagle was first elected mayor at age twenty-one and, despite exposing his problem to his constituents, was overwhelmingly reelected in February 1994. It's a good thing all politicians aren't so eager to get their problems out in the open.

In 1986, the U.S. Forest Service took in $1.3 billion from timber sales but spent $2 billion.

The Smell of English Leather

A strange phenomenon occurred in the mid-sixties. Suddenly cows smelled better. What caused this to occur? Something they were eating? Were they bathing more? Trying to make themselves more appealing to the bulls? No, it seems the Army was up to its old tricks again. In June 1994 the U.S. Army explained to Congress that in 1964 and 1965 scientists had sneaked into stockyards in six different cities and sprayed cattle with deodorant. Was this a bizarre case of pharmaceutical animal testing? No. The Army wanted to discover how easily the Soviets could break into stock-yards and spread hoof-and-mouth disease.

"And now, will y'all stand and be recognized?"
—*Gib Lewis, Texas speaker of the House, on Disability Day, to a group of people in wheelchairs*

I Don't Chew My Cabbage Twice

"The theories—the ideas she expressed about equality of results within legislative bodies and with—by outcome, by decisions made by legislative bodies, ideas related to proportional voting as a general remedy, not in particular cases where the circumstances make that a feasible idea..."

—Vice President Al Gore, on ABC *Nightline,* on why President Clinton withdrew Lani Guinier's nomination to the EEOC

Ballots for the Nashville, Tennessee, 1995 mayoral election included votes for: Moe, Curly, Larry, Joe, and "Shrimp" Stooge.

He Said/She Said

Can you imagine a coed prison? Men and women in lockup, sharing the same cells? It's ridiculous, it's unheard of, it's not true . . . yet. But it could be soon—and we'll be paying for it. In December 1994 New York State Representative Michael Nozzolio announced the state spends $700,000 a year on estrogen for eighty-seven male prisoners who wish to become female. A state law established a right to continue hormone treatments if the person was receiving injections before arrest and imprisonment. I'm sure that comes as good news to some prison inmates, but it concerns some legislators—not because it's a frightening waste of taxpayer money, but because they fear some transsexuals might commit crimes in order to receive free treatments. From cell mate to soul mate; all at the taxpayers expense.

During the late 1980s the EPA was spending over seven dollars on overhead for each dollar spent on Superfund cleanups.

Looking for a Few Good Men

In 1995 Elbert Lewis of Odessa, Texas, received a notice that he had recently failed to register with the Selective Service System on his eighteenth birthday, as required by law. What was this slacker's excuse? At the time Lewis received the notice he was eighty-two years old, had faithfully served in World War II, and had turned eighteen in 1932.

$34,645,000 approved by Congress for research into screwworms, even though the worm has been eliminated from the United States.

Spoiled Sport

Congress spent $17,400,000 for civilian sporting events in 1996 alone. And despite the fact that a lot of sporting events generate a profit ($66 million profit from the 1994 World Cup Soccer games, for example), the Senate rejected an amendment requiring that the government be reimbursed for its expenses in supporting profitable civilian sporting events. Congress doesn't collect what it is owed and continuously overspends—I wonder why they can't balance the budget?

$23 million, by the post office, to find out how long it takes for the mail to be delivered.

A Political Beast of Burden

Boston Curtis will go down in history as the most unlikely of political candidates. The mayor of Milton, Washington, Kenneth Simmons, placed Curtis on the ballot for the Republican precinct committee in 1933, without Curtis's knowledge. Stubborn creature that he was, Curtis refused to campaign, gave no speeches, and made no promises. He was considered a "dark horse" candidate but won the election anyway. His victory made national news because not only was Curtis the underdog—he was also a mule. That's not a new political party; Boston Curtis was an actual mule; his hoofprints were even stamped on his filing notice. Mayor Simmons announced he had endorsed and sponsored the mule's candidacy "to show how careless many voters are." Now how could any self-respecting relative of a donkey join the Republican party?

$1 million for a Utah program to study how to safely cross the street.

2001: A Space Idiodyssey

Menacing stone monoliths. Concrete spikes soaring to seventy feet. A maze of sharp pyramids. A vast map of the earth with stone spikes at various locations. What are they trying to do, scare us? Well, not us. Thirteen experts devised these *Planet of the Apes* warning signals to scare future generations from sites where nuclear waste is stored. The Department of Energy is spending $200,000 to determine the best way to frighten off successive generations. Approximately 300,000 barrels of plutonium-contaminated by-products (retrieved from nuclear weapons factories) will be sealed away inside salt caverns near Carlsbad, New Mexico. Even though the drums will be buried two thousand feet below the surface, they will remain hazardously radioactive for ten thousand years. The Department of Energy worries that a future someone might inadvertently drill into a site, causing a nuclear catastrophe; hence the menacing stone monoliths, sharp spikes, and eerie earthworks. However, knowing how humans hate to be told what to do, some experts disapprove of the scary stone structures. The experts who do think these "scare tactics" will work should consider the Egyptian warnings on tombs, the Inca warnings in temples, and the Myan warnings all carved in stone, which can be found in museums. My thought is, just bury the nuclear waste under Steamtown USA; nobody goes there anyway.

OTHER SOURCES

Newspapers and Periodicals
The American Spectator
Associated Press
Chicago
Chicago Tribune
Cityview (Central Iowa's Independent Weekly)
Esquire
Forbes
Icon (Iowa City Newsweekly)
Life
Los Angeles Times
Maclean's
Metroland Magazine (The Capital Region's Alternative Newsweekly)
Minnesota's Journal of Law and Politics
Nashville Scene
The New Republic
Newsweek
The New York Times
Playboy
The Progressive
The Providence Journal-Bulletin
Providence Phoenix
Reader's Digest
Shooting
Strange Days #1: The Year in Weirdness (1996)
Texas Monthly
Time
U.S. News and World Report
The Wall Street Journal
The Washington Post

Books and Public Documents

Bathroom Readers Institute Staff. *Uncle John's Second Bathroom Reader.* New York: St. Martin's Press, 1989.

————. *Uncle John's Fourth Bathroom Reader.* New York: St. Martin's Press, 1991.

————. *Uncle John's Seventh Bathroom Reader.* Berkeley: Earth Works, 1994.

Boller, Paul F., Jr. *Congressional Anecdotes.* New York: Oxford University Press, 1992.

Bovard, James. *Shakedown: How the Government Screws You from A to Z.* New York: Viking Penguin, 1995.

Committee on Standards of Official Conduct. *Historical Summary of Conduct Cases in the House of Representatives.* Washington, D.C.: U.S. Government Printing Office, April 1992.

Gore, Al. *Creating a Government That Works Better and Costs Less: The Report of the National Performance.* New York: NAL-Dutton, 1993.

Gross, Martin L. *Call for Revolution: How Washington Is Strangling America—and How to Stop It.* New York: Ballantine Books, 1993.

————. *The Government Racket: Washington Waste from A to Z.* New York: Bantam Books, 1992.

————. *The Political Racket: Deceit, Self-interest, and Corruption in American Politics.* New York: Ballantine Books, 1995.

Howard, Phillip K. *The Death of Common Sense.* New York: Random House, 1995.

Kelly, Brian. *Adventures in Porkland: How Washington Wastes Your Money.* New York: Random House, 1992.

Kirchner, Paul. *Oops! A Stupefying Survey of Goofs, Blunders, and Botches, Great and Small.* Santa Monica: General Publishing Group, 1996.

Kohut, John J. *Stupid Government Tricks: Outrageous (but True!) Stories of Bureaucratic Bungling and Washington Waste.* New York: NAL-Dutton, 1995.

————, and Roland Sweet. *Dumb, Dumber, Dumbest: True News of the World's Least Competent People.* New York: NAL-Dutton, 1996.

————, and Roland Sweet. *News from the Fringe: True Stories of Strange People and Stranger Times.* New York: NAL-Dutton, 1993.

Louis, David. *2,201 Fascinating Facts.* Avenal, N.J.: Random House Value Publishing, 1988.

Olive, David. *More Political Babble: The Dumbest Things Politicians Ever Said.* New York: John Wiley & Sons, 1996.

————. *Political Babble: The One Thousand Dumbest Things Ever Said by Politicians.*

New York: John Wiley & Sons, 1992.

O'Neil, Frank. *The Mammoth Book of Oddities*. New York: Carroll & Graf, 1996.

Petras, Kathryn, and Ross Petras. *The 776 Stupidest Things Ever Said*. New York: Doubleday, 1993.

Petras, Ross, and Kathryn Petras. *The 176 Stupidest Things Ever Done*. New York: Doubleday, 1996.

———. *The 776 Even Stupider Things Ever Said*. New York: HarperCollins, 1994.

Proxmire, William. *The Fleecing of America*. Boston: Houghton Mifflin, 1980.

Shepherd, Chuck, John J. Kohut, and Roland Sweet. *News of the Weird*. New York: NAL-Dutton, 1989.

———. *More News of the Weird*. New York: NAL-Dutton, 1990.

———. *Beyond News of the Weird*. New York: NAL-Dutton, 1991.

Shook, Michael D., and Robert L. Shook. *Book of Odds: Winning the Lottery, Finding True Love, Losing Your Teeth, and Other Chances in Day-to-Day Life*. New York: NAL-Dutton, 1993.

"Well, shit!"

—Former Metro Nashville Councilman Ludye Wallace expressing his feelings on live TV about losing his 1995 reelection campaign to Julius Sloss

Send your stories of government goofs to the author at govgoofs@aol.com.